YORKSH
WAL.
– On The Level

Norman Buckley

Published by Sigma Leisure – an imprint of
Sigma Press, 5 Alton Road, Wilmslow, Cheshire SK9 5DY, England.

British Library Cataloguing in Publication Data
A CIP record for this book is available from the British Library.

ISBN: 1-85058-439-7

Typesetting and Design by: Sigma Press, Wilmslow, Cheshire.

Maps: Jeremy Semmens

Cover: the author on a track near Kettlewell, Wharfedale *(June Buckley)*

Printed by: Progress Press Company Ltd.

Disclaimer: the information in this book is given in good faith and is believed to be correct at the time of publication. No responsibility is accepted by either the author or publisher for errors or omissions, or for any loss or injury howsoever caused. Only you can judge your own fitness, competence and experience. Do not rely solely on sketch maps for navigation: we strongly recommend the use of appropriate Ordnance Survey (or equivalent) maps.

Preface

The high tops, rugged moorland, and steep valley sides of the Yorkshire Dales dictate that most circular walks will, in whole or in part, involve steep and long ascents and descents, possibly beyond the capability or desire of many who would otherwise like to spend time walking in this beautiful area.

As was suggested in the first volume in this series, "Lakeland Walking – on the Level", age, and/or disability may necessitate walking on more level ground than was previously the case. Similarly, families with young children, or those from an urban environment who mistrust high, wild, and remote places, may prefer more gentle excursions. Alternatively, it might just be a day when time is short or when the clouds obscure the higher ground.

For whatever reasons, good circular walks which do not involve serious ascent but which explore the heart of the Dales countryside will always be popular; this book selects 32 of the best, all related to popular centres, and offers them with a wealth of interesting features encountered along the way.

The word "level" is, of course, not used in a literal sense, but rather to indicate that the absence of long or steep uphill sections has been the first criterion for inclusion in the book. Most importantly, the total ascent in quantified at the start of each walk, together with the distance, advice whether any ascent is steep and concentrated or is gradual and divided into several sections, and the conditions underfoot. All these criteria contribute in assessing the overall strenuousness of a suggested route.

Not least because Dales farming land can rapidly become muddy underfoot, the use of boots is strongly recommended even for the shortest of these generally easy walks. Because the "level" walker will expect to proceed at a leisurely pace, taking photographs and admiring the fine scenery, the availability of refreshments and/or good picnic areas is of sufficient importance to be mentioned where appropriate.

Assuming that the great majority of walkers will use a motor vehicle to and from the relevant town or village, car parking areas are carefully selected and recommended. Whilst the sketch maps included in the book, taken in conjunction with the text, are fine for following the route, the use of a detailed Ordnance Survey map, as described with each walk, does add to the overall appreciation of the countryside.

Norman Buckley

Which Maps to Use?

Almost all of the walks in this book are covered by the Ordnance Survey 'Outdoor Leisure' series. The only exception is Walk 20, which uses OS 'Pathfinder' maps which are being phased out in favour of the newer 'Explorer' series. At the time of this update, an 'Explorer' for Walk 20 was not available, but it should appear during 2001. If you need this map, please enquire at your local OS stockist.

Contents

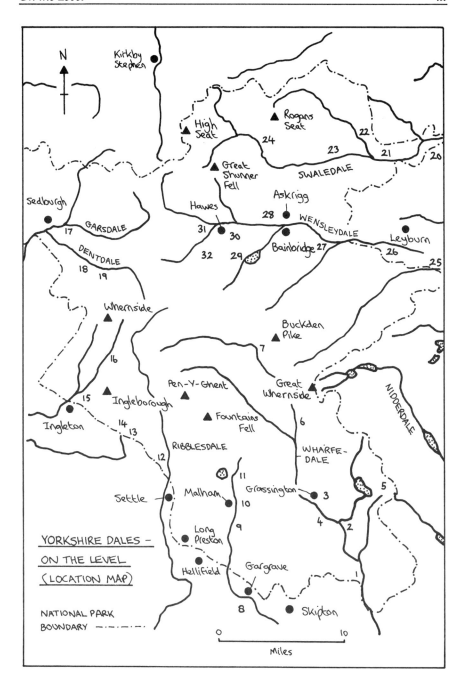

I

Bolton Abbey & Bolton Estate

Length: 7½ miles (with 5½ mile option)

Rise and Fall: Approximately 480 feet total ascent, well-spread and mainly in four separate lengths. Gradients are generally reasonable. Should two riverside sections that are at present closed be re-opened, the total would be greatly reduced.

Underfoot: Mostly very good indeed – grassy and gravelled track, with just a short distance on rougher stone.

Car Parking: Barden Bridge – plenty of free roadside parking or one of the Bolton Estate car parks. (Tickets can be used on the same day in any other of the Estate car parks). Grid reference: 052574

Map: Ordnance Survey Outdoor Leisure No. 10, Yorkshire Dales, Southern area. 1:25000.

Description

This walk is almost entirely within the Bolton Estate, owned by the Duke and Duchess of Devonshire (the Cavendish family). It encompasses an outstanding stretch of Wharfedale, with the steep, often rocky, valley sides largely clothed with woodland. Although this is managed woodland, there is no real appearance of artificiality as the preponderance of varied hardwood species, sycamore and beech being paramount, has an entirely natural aspect.

Strid Wood is designated as a Site of Special Scientific Interest and a Wildlife Conservation Area, with several waymarked Nature Trails having a good variety of flora and fauna. Information on these and other aspects of the Estate is available at the Cavendish Pavilion.

Close to the start is the Barden Tower, the ruin of an old hunting lodge, enlarged in 1485, restored in 1658 by the redoubtable Lady Anne Clifford, and now part of the Estate. Refreshments, including light meals, are served in the adjacent Priest House. Barden Bridge is an old West Yorkshire County bridge of 1676.

Despite all these good things, the climax of the walk is undoubtedly Bolton Priory (more usually referred to as Bolton Abbey), the impressive remains of a 12th century Augustinian foundation, beautifully set by the river. Fortunately the last Prior managed to save the nave from destruction

Stepping stones over River Wharfe at Bolton Priory

at the Dissolution in 1539. It survives as the Parish Church of St Mary and St Cuthbert.

Another of the great attractions of Wharfedale is the Strid, a gorge only a few feet wide through which the whole of the River Wharf pours. In places the depth exceeds 30 feet and the millstone grit has been gouged and undercut by pebbles and grit in suspension. Leaping across the Strid has been known but is definitely not recommended; it is said that nobody has ever failed twice in attempting this leap!

This walk follows the route of the Dales Way long distance footpath for much of the distance, plus various well-used and marked nature trails. It makes a fine circuit but, with a fair amount of up and down, it should not be underestimated.

Bolton Priory

Route

Start at Barden Bridge. Go through a gate on the north-east side (the left bank of the river), at the entrance to the Estate car park. A well-trod path crosses the riverside meadows, soon reaching one end of an imposingly castellated bridge, which is actually an ornamented aqueduct of the former Bradford

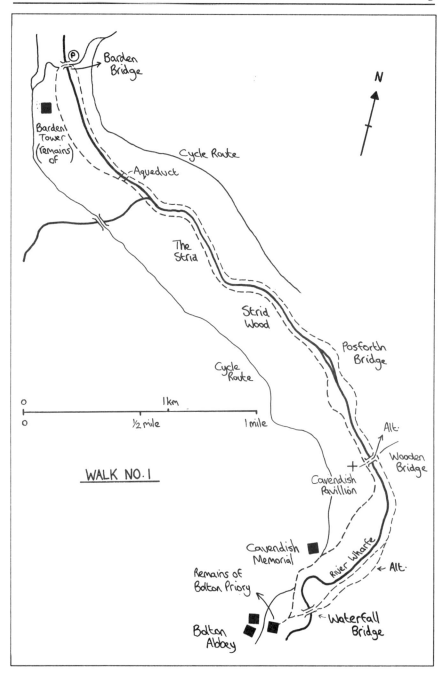

WALK NO.1

Corporation Waterworks. The track continues to the first, gentle, ascent as it enters Strid Wood. The path now keeps well above the river, rather up and down along the steep valley side. There are seats well-placed with views of the famous Strid and, at the crest of this particular section, a well-constructed shelter.

The way now descends, along the side of a minor road for a short distance near Posforth Bridge, to reach the river bank and a level section to the Wooden Bridge. Across the river is the Cavendish Pavilion, with refreshments, public conveniences, information centre, and shop.

Unless this is far enough, or there are dire needs, don't cross the river, but follow the signpost "Bolton Priory 1". On reaching woodland, at a stile turn left to rejoin the minor road at a ford. As the former, lower, path has been closed by the Estate Management, go uphill for 40 yards and then fork right along the official path formed by the Estate. There is quite a climb in two main sections. However, there is also a branching path to the right in approximately a quarter of a mile, angling down steeply to the river and then following the bank to reach the large grassy area near the Priory. This possible alternative avoids the second main part of the ascent, a steepish 40 feet or so.

By whatever route, the Waterfall Bridge and stepping stones, flat topped and regularly spaced, are reached. This part of the Estate is a great weekend and holiday family playground, with a partially sandy river beach. Cross the river to the Priory and bear right, uphill, to the road, turning right to follow the roadside footpath to the Cavendish Memorial, a fairly undistinguished 19th century monument. Turn right to descend steps and a steep little slope, cross the riverside meadow, and follow the surfaced roadway close to the river as far as the Cavendish Pavilion.

The route re-enters Strid Wood along a track which has been eased for wheelchair use. At a triple fork take the middle, widest, track, soon reaching a clearing with information board and then the Strid itself, a short detour to the right. Continue with a short but steep uphill stretch, following signs to "Strid Car Park and Barden Bridge", some of the path now being rough underfoot. At a fork (with signpost) keep right for Barden Bridge, soon descending to river level and reaching the aqueduct.

The way now stays close to the river, partly in the open and partly in another woodland plantation, all the way to the bridge. A sign gives the date of this plantation as 1894 and it is interesting to observe the extent of growth of the various species of trees in the succeeding 100 years.

<u>2</u>

Wharfedale: Appletreewick and Skyreholme

Length: 6½ miles.

Rise and Fall: With a total ascent of 550 feet, this is one of the more strenuous walks in the book. From the start to the Grassington to Pateley Bridge road, the route is generally uphill, mostly at a reasonable gradient, but with one quite steep section. Having achieved this height, the level is maintained for a considerable distance until the drop to Appletreewick. The other, lesser, ascent is from the River Wharfe back to Skyreholme, steady rather than steep.

Underfoot: First rate paths throughout; less than one mile on public road.

Car Parking: By the bridge at Middle Skyreholme there is space for three or four vehicles at the side of the cul de sac road to Higher Skyreholme. There are further informal roadside spaces on the road leading to Parceval Hall.

Map: Ordnance Survey Outdoor Leisure No. 10 Yorkshire Dales, Southern area. 1 : 25000

Mock Beggar Hall, Appletreewick

Troller's Gill

Description

This is such a fine, varied, walk that it carries a high recommendation despite the considerable ascent. The parking place is close to Parceval Hall, where the highly regarded gardens are open to the public throughout a long season, and a visit can readily be combined with the walk.

Appletreewick is a village of great antiquity, having no less than three long established halls, High, Low, and the quaintly named Mock Beggar, all by the roadside and readily seen by the passer-by. The church was converted from two cottages, one of them the birth place in 1548 of Sir William Craven, an esteemed local benefactor who, like Dick Whittington, packed his bags for London at a young age, later rising to become Lord Mayor. There are also two inns, each with tempting outside tables having wonderful views across the dale.

The riverside footpath below Appletreewick is among the best in Wharfedale, winding past rushing rapids with steep, superbly wooded, banks.

Route

From the bridge over Skyreholme Beck turn right to ascend the Parceval Hall access road, signposted "Parceval Hall ½". Just before the wooden bridge where the Parceval Hall gardens are entered, turn left at a farm gate signposted "Gill Heads 1, and New Road". A well-used grassy track heads for another farm gate, then through a stile with small gate.

After passing the Parceval Hall woodland, the valley becomes an attractive mini dale with plenty of limestone showing on the hillsides. After a ladder stile is what appears to be a broken dam, with a depression which must have been a reservoir at some time in the past. The path terraces along the valley side to another stile and a junction with an information board.

To the right is Trollers Gill, a fine rocky defile, now threaded by a permissive footpath. [This can be used as an alternative route, but there is a steep little climb of about 50 feet at the top end in rejoining the main path, and the Gill is rough underfoot. There is also a legendary spectral hound, credited with frightening at least one local resident to death]

The main route goes left at the junction; here is the steepest climb, getting on for 150 feet over a short distance. However, the path is very good and, although the valley is less spectacular than Trollers Gill, there is the interest of old mining levels and some other evidence of former workings. Above this area a small footpath on the right is the connecting route from Trollers Gill.

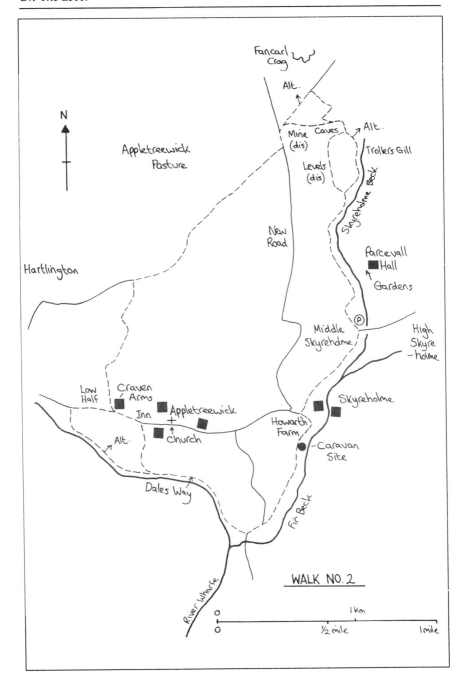

WALK NO. 2

The route is now along an old mine roadway bearing round to the left, with plenty of shake holes evident. Immediately before the roadway swings right to climb the slope opposite, look out for a minor footpath on the left which cuts off a corner, joining New Road at a ladder stile. If this path is missed, the roadway is followed to its junction with New Road, opposite Fancarl Crag.

Approximately 100 yards after the road bends to the left, turn right at a farm gate to take a broad, stony, track, signposted "Hartlington ¾" for a level tramp across wild moorland, in total contrast to the first part of the walk. The views are right across Wharfedale as the long descent begins gradually. The wild moor is left at a farm gate with a stile; the same track continues downhill, eventually bearing right through a farm gate. In a further 80 yards, immediately before a second farm gate, turn left at an "Appletreewick" signpost.

Another farm trackway now provides an unmistakeable route, with just one slight rise, all the way to Appletreewick. A few ash and conifer trees are passed and the last section is an unsurfaced lane, falling steeply to emerge by the side of the Craven Arms inn, with the old village stocks adjacent. Turn left along the road for a quarter of a mile. At the near end of the village proper is the New inn, a little further are the old halls, church, and other fine buildings.

Opposite the New inn is a private road to the river, with a requested 10p. contribution from pedestrians. Unless the public footpath, which is almost half a mile to the west, is preferred, take this private roadway. Turn left at the river bank, along the Dales Way (yet again!) and follow this delightful route as far as a minor road by a bridge.

Turn left along the road and, as it bends left, go over a stile on the right signposted "Skyreholme". The path is barely evident, fairly close to the wall. As the wall ends, bear a little left, keeping above the steep sided valley of the Fir Beck. Go over a hump, pass well to the right of a field barn, then follow the line of a fence to a stile. Pass above a valley bottom static caravan site to a stile and then follow the site access roadway to Howarth Farm, turning left up to the road.

Turn right to pass through Skyreholme hamlet before reaching the road junction and the car parking area.

3

Grassington Moor

Length: 3 miles (full circuit)

Rise and Fall: Almost 400 feet (full circuit), mainly in two sections. The alternative return route reduces this total by about 100 feet.

Underfoot: Very good. Stony tracks for almost all the way.

Car Parking: Roadside verges at Yarnbury, 1¾ miles above Grassington. Grid reference: 015659.

Map: Ordnance Survey Outdoor Leisure No. 30, Yorkshire Dales, Northern and Central areas. 1:25000.

Description

This short walk provides the rare opportunity for a circuit on high moorland (the chimney stands at 1235 feet) without any really strenuous ascent. The moor is bleak and windswept and the scenery could hardly be described as pretty. Grand, perhaps, but much modified by man, as extensive mining, with some quarrying, have produced vast quantities of spoil, dominating the landscape. This, then, is a walk very much for those with an interest in industrial history. Grassington Moor was a thriving centre of the Wharfedale lead industry which, like that of Swaledale, ebbed and flowed over many centuries, probably from Roman times. The great period here was the early 19th century, when the Duke of Devonshire invested heavily in the industry, installing a great deal of new plant, powered by water wheels fed by an intricate system of waterways and reservoirs. There is still much to be seen and part of the moor is now the "Grassington Moor Lead Mines Conservation Area". Discreet information boards along the way help the visitor to interpret the remains of this once great industry.

Route

From the car parking area at Yarnbury, leave Moor Lane at a gate on the right with a "bridleway to Hebden" sign. You are at once in an area of land still showing all the scars of its past disturbance. Up to the left are several of the information boards and, in wet weather, a pond is formed on the site of a former reservoir. Proceed along the broad stony track, which has the rather

Grassington Moor: chimney of former smelter

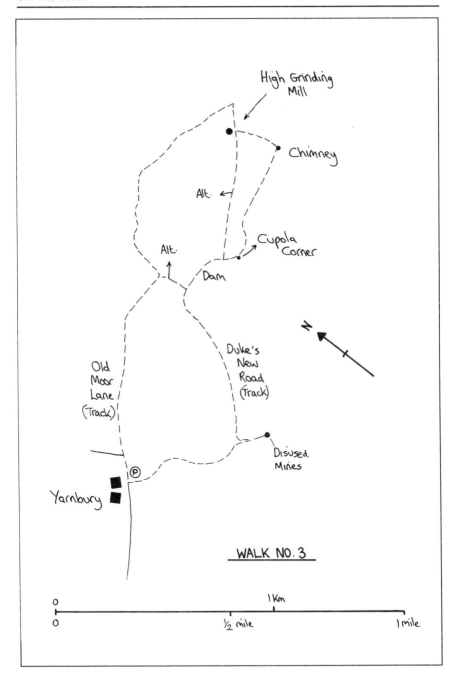

High Grinding Mill

Chimney

Alt.

Cupola Corner

Alt.

Dam

N

Duke's New Road (Track)

Old Moor Lane (Track)

Disused Mines

Ⓟ

Yarnbury

WALK NO. 3

0

0

1 Km

½ mile

1 mile

grand title of "Duke's New Road", dating from the early 19th century revival of the industry by the Duke of Devonshire.

On the right of the track are good examples of "bell pits", resulting from earlier, more primitive, methods of mining the lead ore. Divert along a grassy path on the right to Beevor Dam, now a reedy pool, close to the remains of extensive works which include the deep Union shaft.

Grassington Moor: lead mining remains

Return to the main roadway, which descends a little to cross a high dam before climbing gently to a ladder stile and the remains of the Cupola Smelt Mill, a 1793 replacement of an earlier mill on the same site. Above the mill, fork right to rise steadily towards the impressive chimney on the skyline. A grassy track follows the line of the main flue which, leading to the chimney, vented the toxic combustion products from the mill. There was a complex arrangement of these flues permitting condensation of the gases and the regulation of flue gas temperatures. Partial collapses of the roofs of some flues allow the fine construction to be admired. The restored chimney is soon reached.

Turn left (no footpath) to cross the grassy ground towards the ruined structures of High Grinding Mill, where the 1955-61 re-working of the waste dumps for fluorite and barite is revealed by the remains of modern building materials.

[For the easiest return to Yarnbury, turn left to follow the Duke's New Road all the way back].

For a slightly longer walk, turn right up the road and then left at a junction of four similar roadways. Follow this track as it dips into a dry valley, climbing steadily before becoming Old Moor Lane and descending to Yarnbury. [If the rise ahead is daunting, a footpath on the left at a gate and stile provides a short link back to the Duke's New Road for a more level return] By the side of the lane at Yarnbury, the portal of Barratt's incline of 1828 is still obvious; close by, the wall shows evidence of the line of the former tramway of about the same date.

Cottages at Grassington

4

Grassington & Hebden

Length: 4½ miles

Rise and Fall: Total ascent approximately 280 feet, 60% of which is in the rise at the start of the walk, from the car park through Grassington village to High Lane. Most of the remainder is at the end, from the river to the car park. Gradients are never severe.

Underfoot: Excellent throughout. Only a little is on public roads.

Car parking: Public car Park, Grassington. Grid reference: 002638

Map: Ordnance Survey Outdoor Leisure No. 30 Yorkshire Dales, Northern and Central areas. 1: 25000

Description

Grassington is a fine village, the "capital" of middle/upper Wharfedale, with cottages, shops, and inns jumbled in a most pleasing mixture around its little square. Even the public car park is attractive, with picnic tables on grassy areas and a modern Tourist Information Centre. In fact, tourism has obviously taken over from lead mining (see Walk 3) as the leading local industry. However, the local history is displayed for all to see in the Upper Wharfedale Folk Museum in the village square.

Hebden is a modest village, another former lead mining centre, with inn, shop, and some attractive cottages. The walk is very varied throughout its short length and gives an excellent taste of the delights of upper Wharfedale.

Route

From the car park turn left along the road to the village centre, turn right at Main Street and follow this thoroughfare to its top by the Old Town Hall. There are plenty of shops to look at on the way, perhaps distracting attention from the continuous ascent. Turn sharp right at the top, then fork left (cul de sac road), still uphill. Turn left again into High Lane at a "Hebden" signpost. The end of the long rise is near as the stony lane soon levels out.

As the lane terminates at a stile, the path goes straight on across meadow land, fairly well-worn and clear on the ground. Further stiles and "footpath" signposts and a short woodland traverse lead to a complex of disused

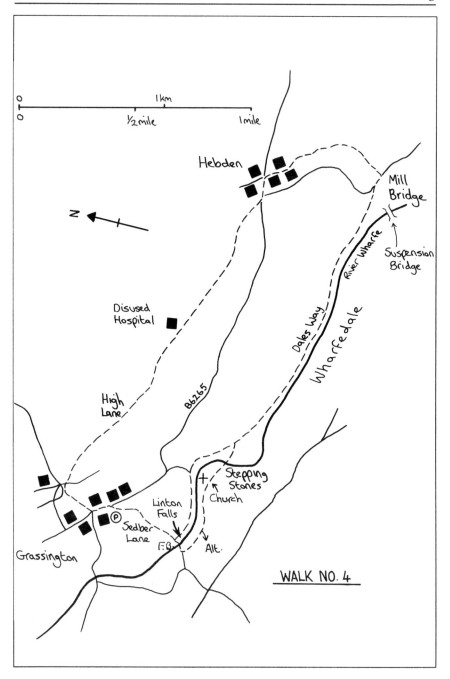

buildings with a tall brick chimney, a former isolation hospital. By the corner of the first building a signpost "Hebden" points the way across a grassy expanse.

Continue over further stiles, ignoring an inviting farm track. Hebden and its church come into view ahead as the track descends gently to a stile and walled lane leading to the public road. Turn left, pass the Clarendon Hotel (bar meals etc.), and turn right into the village street. Immediately after passing the school turn left at an old kissing gate with a "Hebden Suspension Bridge ½" signpost, and descend to the side of the stream. Ignore the footbridge and continue through a stile with gate, then a kissing gate, and cross a footbridge by a weir, which must have been associated with a former mill. Pass the sewage works, to a four-armed signpost and follow "Hebden Suspension Bridge" to a small gate, descending between houses to a minor road.

Turn right for a few yards, cross Mill Bridge, and then turn left through a gate with a "Grassington Bridge 2" signpost, angling across to join the riverside path, which is part of the Dales Way long distance footpath. A short diversion to the left gives a closer view of the pedestrian suspension bridge and the stepping stones which presumably had to suffice before the bridge was built. Few would now venture to cross by the older method!

The Dales Way provides an easy and delightful route along the side of the river, generally tranquil and with a line of mature trees, largely horse chestnut. No route finding, no rough ground underfoot, just a gentle ramble in pleasant surroundings.

St Michael's Church at Linton comes into view across the river. This is the oldest church in the area and for centuries worshippers from Hebden had to travel by this same path, crossing the river on stepping stones. [An interesting diversion here is to cross the river, (but not after prolonged heavy rain), visiting Linton Church, and continuing along the minor road to the former mill complex, then turning right over the footbridge to reach Sedber Lane].

The main route turns right through a gate, follows a lane for a short distance, then turning left over a stile at a "Grassington and Linton Falls" signpost. Go across meadows with further stiles; the roar of the falls becomes more distinct, while across the river the substantial former mill complex (woollen, cotton, and corn), last used in 1959, has been tastefully rebuilt into dwellings. The footbridge over the river is a good viewpoint for the great weirs, indicative of the size and importance of these former mills.

However, to return to Grassington, the turn from the path is to the right, then uphill along Sedber Lane, an interesting old mill access route, narrow between its flanking walls. The unfortunate asphalt skimming over the original paving slabs is now, happily, wearing away. A gate on the left leads directly into the car park.

Linton church and stepping stones

5

Wharfedale: Grimwith Reservoir Circular

Length: 5 miles.

Rise and Fall: about 130 feet. No steep gradients. Apart from the slight rise at the start, and the return to the car park, this is just about as level walking as can be found.

Underfoot: Generally good.

Car Parking: Pay and display car park operated by Yorkshire Water, reached by the Water Authority road from the B6265 Grassington to Pateley Bridge road.

Map: Ordnance Survey Outdoor Leisure No. 10 Yorkshire Dales, Southern area. 1 : 25000.

Description

This is very much a walk for lovers of wide open spaces, as the reservoir is surrounded by open moorland, rough sheep-grazing country without trees, although the Water Authority has carried out some planting adjacent to the car park. There is also a lack of scarps, quarries, or other significant landscape features, only Grimwith House, a few barns, the odd bridge, and a large dam showing evidence of human impact on this wild countryside.

However, the reservoir is not unattractive. Its irregular shape and a less than usually unsightly draw-down line contribute to making this walk worthwhile. In addition to the public conveniences, there are picnic tables by the car park.

Route

As the Water Authority has allowed permissive footpaths to link with existing rights of way, the route around the reservoir is very straightforward. From the car park turn right, uphill, along a stony roadway. In less than a quarter of a mile turn left at a signpost "Yorkshire Water waterside footpath". A good path winds downhill to the side of the water, eventually rejoining the roadway, which is then followed along the shore.

When the roadway ends, the route continues as a footpath, close to the water. To cross Gate Up Gill, the approved route keeps well to the right and is at some distance from the reservoir until after the next stream, Blea Gill, is crossed. Just after passing Far Rams Close, the start of Hartingtons Moor

is crossed. Just after passing Far Rams Close, the start of Hartingtons Moor Lane is reached; turn left to follow the footpath to the western end of the dam. From the top of the dam are probably the best views of the whole circuit, including Simon's Seat, Carncliffe Top, and Burnsall and Thorpe Fell. The return from the dam to the car park is the only ascent of any significance.

Grimwith reservoir

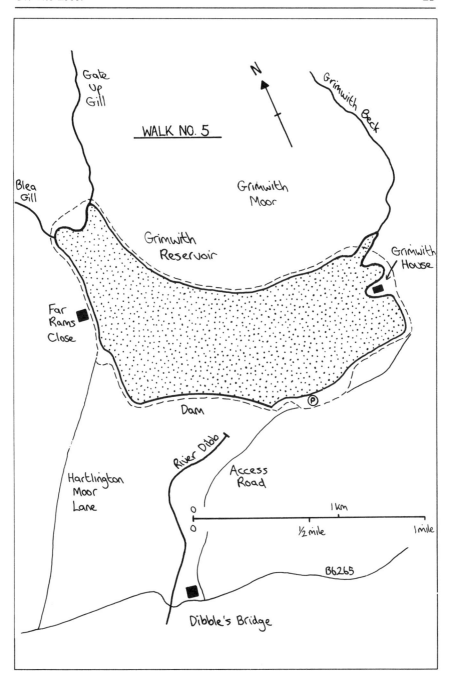

Gate Up Gill

Grimwith Beck

WALK NO. 5

N

Grimwith Moor

Blea Gill

Grimwith Reservoir

Grimwith House

Far Rams Close

Dam

P

River Dibb

Access Road

Hartlington Moor Lane

1 km

½ mile

1 mile

B6265

Dibble's Bridge

Footbridge over the River Wharfe

6

Wharfedale: Kettlewell and Starbotton

Length: 4¼ miles

Rise and Fall: Approximately 270 feet; the only significant ascent is the initial climb from Kettlewell.

Underfoot: Generally very good footpaths; just a few sections have a rougher surface.

Car Parking: Pay and display car park, Kettlewell village. Grid reference: 969724.

Map: Ordnance Survey Outdoor Leisure No. 30 Yorkshire Dales, Northern and Central areas. 1:25000

Description

Kettlewell and Starbotton are two of the best known and most popular villages of upper Wharfedale. Both are pleasantly stone-built with bright cottage gardens softening the somewhat austere beauty of this part of the dale. Early occupation of the area is evident from the field systems on the hillside above Kettlewell, whilst in medieval times Fountains Abbey, with its important grange at nearby Kilnsey, was a major power in the valley. Other monastic houses at Coverham and Bolton also had land holdings in the vicinity; because of this religious complexity, for many years Kettlewell church was served by two priests.

Whilst Grassington was the most important lead mining centre in Wharfedale, the industry also affected Kettlewell, several of its dwellings having originated as miners' cottages. Long ago a market town, it is now just a village but, as a tourist centre, it is provided with three inns, tea shops, stores and public conveniences.

Starbotton was devastated by floods in 1686, following which almost total rebuilding of the village was necessary; many of the buildings of this period remain today. There is one inn.

The present walk provides a very pleasant and easy circuit linking these two attractive villages.

Route

From the car park turn left into Kettlewell, crossing the bridge over Dowber Gill Beck and passing between the competing hostelries – the Racehorses and the Bluebell. Turn right by the side of the Bluebell and, as the surfaced road bends right, carry straight on, rising up a stony track by Cam Lodge, followed by a footpath signposted "Starbotton 1¾".

Go over a stile with gate, still rising, and follow a well-worn grassy track, turning left as it levels out. The hard work of the walk is now over as an unmistakeable path keeps more or less the same height on the valley side practically all the way to Starbotton. Below is the intake wall, separating the better quality farming land from the rough, boulder-strewn, grazing which reaches high to the moor above. Until the plantation near Starbotton is reached, trees are sparse along the way, generally a few good ash and some old hawthorns.

There are ladder stiles and a few minor ups and downs but, in general this is a fine footpath with great views both along and across the dale to the high plateau of Old Cote Moor Top.

Close to Starbotton a "footpath" signpost points the way to another yellow-capped post and then a further signpost, where a left turn over a stile precedes a steep descent to the road. Turn right to the village, including the Fox and Hounds Inn.

The return route leaves the village at the Kettlewell end, by a right turn through a farm gate into an unsurfaced lane, signposted (inter alia) "Kettlewell 2". The river is crossed by a footbridge (good picnic site by the riverside); turn left over a stile signposted "Kettlewell", and proceed along the edge of a meadow. The route, which is part of the Dales Way, soon becomes clear on the ground; although it is basically a riverside footpath, it does diverge to the right in places, the first being in less than a quarter of a mile, as it cuts across the neck of several meanders.

Although a little rough underfoot in places, the Way provides an excellent level return to Kettlewell, requiring no route-finding and with only a few stiles. As the car park comes into view, bear right to rise to the road, then turning left over the bridge.

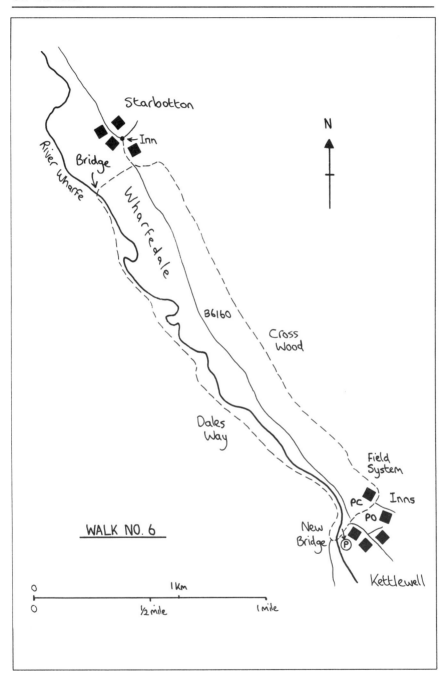

Starbotton

Inn

River Wharfe

Bridge

Wharfedale

B6160

Cross Wood

Dales Way

N

Field System

Inns

PC

PO

New Bridge

P

Kettlewell

WALK NO. 6

0   1 Km

0   ½ mile   1 mile

Kilnsey Crag near Kettlewell

7

Wharfedale: Buckden and Hubberholme

Length: 7½ miles (shorter version 5¼ miles).

Rise and Fall: Total ascent is a little more than 550 feet, virtually all contained in the long rise from the car park, on a good path and at a steady gradient.

Underfoot: Mostly excellent tracks, but with one or two short, stony, descents. There is half a mile of road walking near Hubberholme.

Car Parking: Pay and display car park in Buckden village. Grid reference: 943773.

Map: Ordnance Survey Outdoor Leisure No. 30 Yorkshire Dales, Northern and Central areas. 1 : 25000.

Description

Buckden is strategically sited close to the head of the true Wharfedale, the valley of the River Wharfe above Hubberholme being known as Langstrothdale. The village is also at the junction of the two roads which climb over the moorland into Wensleydale, left to Hawes, and right to Aysgarth. In medieval times Buckden was the administrative centre of the Percy family's hunting forest of Langstrothdale, the term "forest" in this context having nothing to do with trees.

Yet another distinction is that Buckden, together with its inn, has the highest situated shop in Wharfedale. It is also a very attractive settlement in a part of the valley which must be a favourite of those visitors who prefer the quieter, more remote, higher reaches of the dales to the more commercialised honeypots.

For these various reasons, a visit to Buckden is considered to be essential for Dales walkers, hence the inclusion of the following walk despite the labour of its initial ascent. It is a very fine walk, well worth the effort involved.

However, if for any reason the climb and/or the distance do not appeal, a visit to Buckden is still recommended, with a level walk to Hubberholme (1½ miles), where the George Inn is open all day, and a return by the same route (Dales Way footpath). This walk can be extended to Yockenthwaite and the cairn circle (3½ miles) if desired.

Hubberholme church of St Michael and All Angels is a gem. Formerly a remote forest chapel, it has a good deal of surviving Norman work, a rare and remarkable rood loft of 1558, pews by Thompson of Kilburn with his "mouse" motif, and a genuinely unspoilt, "original" atmosphere overall. The ashes of J.B. Priestley, the great Yorkshire writer, are scattered here.

Half a mile above Yockenthwaite, close to the river, is a "cairn circle", either a Bronze Age stone circle or perhaps a ring of boulders around a small tomb of similar date.

Upper Wharfedale

Route

From the car park make for the farm gate signposted "Buckden Pike, Cray High Bridge" and take the fine, wide, track which climbs remorselessly up the hillside and through Rakes Wood.

Above the sparse woodland the track bends right along Buckden Rake, now at more than 1000 feet above sea level and with marvellous views over a wide span of high moorland. The summit of Buckden Pike – at 2303 feet, one of Yorkshire's highest – is above to the right. The broad, grassy track is beautifully terraced on the hillside. After Cray hamlet comes into view, look for a small gate in the wall on the left signposted "Cray". Turn left and

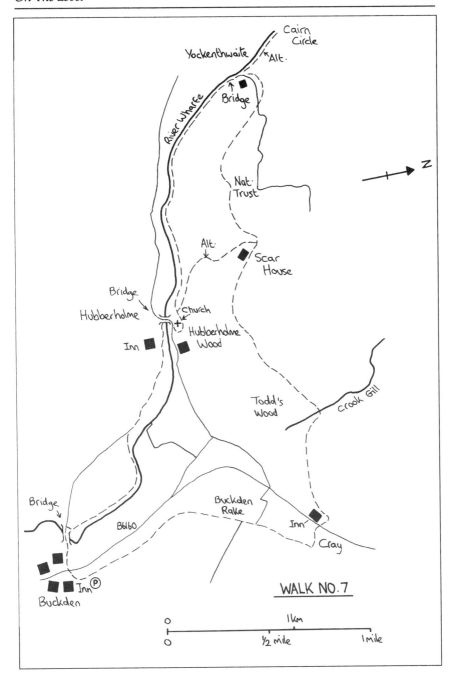

Cairn Circle

Yockenthwaite

Alt.

River Wharfe

Bridge

N

Nat. Trust

Alt.

Scar House

Bridge

Hubberholme

Church

Inn

Hubberholme Wood

Todd's Wood

Crook Gill

Bridge

Buckden Rake

B6160

Inn

Cray

Inn Ⓟ

Buckden

WALK NO. 7

0   1Km

0   ½ mile   1 mile

descend, with care on the slippery stones, to Cray Gill, crossed on easy stepping stones.

Cross the road by the White Lion Inn and follow a signpost "Stubbing Bridge 1, Yockenthwaite 4", along a rising farm track. There has been a footpath diversion here. Keep to the right of the farm buildings, cross a muddy farm yard, pass a "Scar House and Yockenthwaite" sign, and reach open grazing land.

The path is now clear on the ground, with the route confirmed by occasional yellow splodges. It provides a superb level walk for a considerable distance, contouring above the steep limestone scarps, still at more than 1000 feet above sea level. Below is rather sparse woodland which could possibly, at least in part, be a remainder of the ancient afforestation of the dale. A few small areas of exposed clints and grikes add variety.

After the solitude, arrival at Scar House comes almost as a surprise, with a short descent on stones needing care in wet weather.

[Here, the shorter version of the walk requires a sharp left turn to follow the signpost "Hubberholme" for a straightforward descent of the Scar House access roadway to Hubberholme Church].

Our route to Yockenthwaite goes straight on, entering woodland at a stile with gate. The abundance of the non-native sycamore, which grows well at high levels on the Yorkshire Dales limestone, is evidence that this woodland is plantation. A footbridge spans the mini chasm of a dry watercourse, followed by a diagonal left turn, downhill, to a stile.

Yockenthwaite comes into view and a yellow arrow shows the way through a wall on the left, the rough-surfaced path then descending towards the hamlet. At the signpost in Yockenthwaite, turn left for Hubberholme.

[To visit the stone circle turn right towards Deepdale]

Despite another Footpath Diversion Order, the way seems to be straightforward; there is another signpost "Hubberholme" and the path passes to the nearside of the building which is nearest to the river, not between that building and the river. After a small gate, go right to a stile in the wall and descend to the river bank. Once again we are following the Dales Way, keeping close to the river, which has lively rapids and still pools in succession, all pleasantly tree-lined.

At Holme Barns, there is yet another Diversion Order, which has squeezed the path even closer to the river. After passing this section, a left turn to rejoin the old route, well-trodden across a meadow, is necessary. As a steep section of river bank is apparent ahead, the track appears to rise to the left, passing a ruined farm building before joining the Scar House access roadway and descending to Hubberholme Church. However, to avoid the climb, look out for the start of a lesser track on the right, which continues to hug the river bank before passing behind the church to join the Scar House roadway.

Cross the impressively solid bridge towards the George Inn and turn left along the road for half a mile. Turn left at a farm gate with a "Buckden Bridge" signpost and follow a broad riverside path. Rejoin the road at a stile, turning left into the village.

Hubberholme church interior

8

Gargrave and the Leeds and Liverpool Canal

Length: 5 miles

Rise and Fall: 225 feet rise in total, mostly in two modest ascents, one on the Pennine Way, the other on the lane rising to Newton Grange Farm. No steep gradients.

Underfoot: The lane and the canal towpath are excellent and most of the Pennine Way is also very good. Before the farm, the lane is likely to be muddy for a short distance.

Car Parking: Two small free public car parks close to the village hall in Gargrave. Grid reference: 932543/4

Map: Ordnance Survey Outdoor Leisure No. 10 Yorkshire Dales, Southern area. 1 : 25000

Description

Gargrave is a substantial village situated on the River Aire, with all normal amenities but unfortunate in having the main A65 trunk road passing through. There are, however, some attractive features, not least some well-converted barns and other old dwellings along the road south of the river. Another undoubted asset is the station on the renowned Settle and Carlisle railway line.

The Pennine Way is known to all serious walkers as a continuous route linking Edale in Derbyshire with Kirk Yetholm on the Scottish border, its 200+ miles providing a very demanding challenge. This walk gives a rare opportunity for "level" walkers to sample the Pennine Way, albeit in a very modest way.

The Leeds and Liverpool Canal is a trans-Pennine waterway, a "wide" canal 127 miles long linking the docks at Liverpool with the former West Riding of Yorkshire, of great importance in the pre-railway era. The section included in this walk has locks, aqueduct, and bridges. In common with canal structures generally, there is a wonderful coincidence of fitness for purpose with attractive appearance; a towpath walk in this area is anything but dull. All in all, this is a fine and varied walk.

Route

From the car park, walk towards the main road, passing the village hall. On the far side of the main road cross the River Aire by the road bridge and follow Church Road towards the railway station for about a quarter of a mile. Look for a part concealed "Pennine Way" signpost between Church Close House and Pebble Barn.

Turn right here and go over the stone stile on the left, continuing along the side of the house now called "Pennine Way". You are now following this esteemed route. Head for a stile with yellow arrow, bend a little left to another stile, and cross a rising meadow, keeping left of the telegraph poles towards a part concealed stile close to the top left corner.

Turn left along the farm lane at a "Pennine Way" sign, cross the railway, and continue to rise along a stony track with a convenient seat almost at the top of the rise. Canal boats can be seen away to the right; closer at hand is Scaleber farmstead. Above the seat the Way cuts across part of a field towards a prominent post which points the direction to a kissing gate. From here the route is always clear on the ground and each of the several stiles has a yellow arrow. As the path appears to curve to the left, look out for a double stile and plank bridge on the right. Cross this and go up and over a hillock to a stile at a farm lane, close to a stone bridge.

Canal boat at Bank Newton

Turn sharp right to ascend the stony lane and carry on through Newton Grange Farm, after which the lane is surfaced, soon running alongside the canal. Cross the canal and go sharp left over a stile, then left again under the bridge to follow the towpath back towards Gargrave.

From here it is either level, or downhill as the locks are passed, all the way. On a clear day there are long views to the hills north of Skipton. After the flight of locks at Bank Newton, the towpath is lost for a short distance and the adjacent road must be followed to Priest Holme Bridge. At the bridge go down to the right and circle back underneath to regain the towpath. There is an aqueduct carrying the canal over the River Aire, a railway bridge, and three more locks before passing under the main A65 road close to the Anchor Inn.

After the main road, it is less than half a mile to bridge 170, by a lock with a sign giving the distances to important canalside places. Leave the canal here, turning right to return to the car park.

Leeds and Liverpool Canal at Gargrave

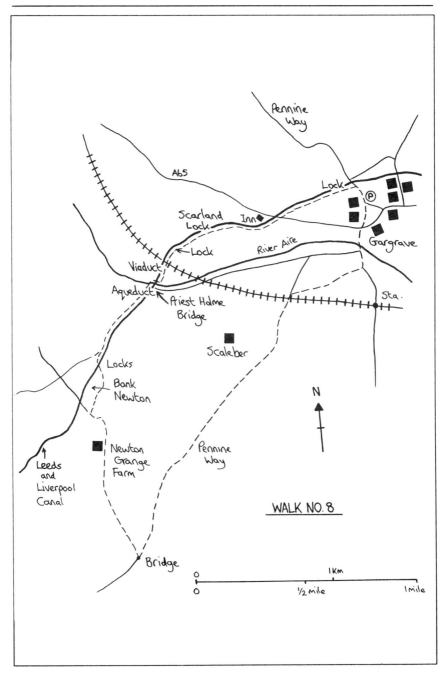

WALK NO. 8

<u>9</u>

Malham to Airton

Length: 7 miles

Rise and Fall: 340 feet, most of which is included in either the initial ascent or the longer climb (190 feet) after Kirkby Malham. Apart from the river bank at Kirkby Malham, gradients are not really steep.

Underfoot: Generally good, but some meadows are without a footpath, less than a mile on public road.

Car Parking: Pay and display public car park, Malham. Grid reference: 900627

Map: Ordnance Survey Outdoor Leisure No. 10, Yorkshire Dales, Southern area. 1 : 25000.

Description

Malham village is described in walk 10, "Malham, Janet's Foss and Gordale Scar". The valley of the River Aire to the south of the village does not have the spectacular limestone features for which the Malham district is famous. It is, however, most attractive in its own, more gentle, way and the path between Kirkby Malham and Airton provides some good upland walking without excessive climbing.

The Buck Inn, Malham village

Kirkby Malham has the 15th century parish church of St Michael, with an 11th century font and the signature of Oliver Cromwell in the register. This church formerly served most of the upper part of Airedale. There is also the Victoria Inn.

Close by is Scalegill Mill, occupying a site in mill use since the 11th century, with a mention in the Domesday Book. Over the centuries this mill has been used for corn, flax, wool, and cotton; there are still operational turbines, generating electricity.

The very old settlement of Airton is attractively grouped around a triangular village green. The house on the green is claimed to be an example of a "squatter house" – land rights were acquired by completing construction of a dwelling and having smoke issuing from the chimney within 24 hours of starting. The absence of an inn in such a substantial village is due to the strong Quaker influence; there is still a Friends Meeting House.

Converted mill at Airton

Route

Leave Malham by the road towards Kirkby Malham; as the road rises, go over an unsignposted stile on the right and angle uphill across the field at about 45 degrees to a stile over the fence ahead. Continue to another stile and stay close to the field boundary. The way is not well-defined on the ground, but goes in a more or less straight line towards a farm building, passed to the right. Angle a little right across the next field to a stile, then another, before veering slightly left to rejoin the road at a fingerpost sign.

Kirkby Malham village is now a short downhill stroll. Turn left to pass the inn, then immediately right before the river. Just past the church entrance, go left to a footbridge over the river, signposted "Otterburn", and climb the far bank, steep but with rudimentary steps.

The climb continues towards the side of, and then alongside, a plantation; at the top, angle left across a huge meadow, aiming for the right-hand end of Deepdale Plantation. By the angle of the walls near that plantation, go right over a stile, up along the side of the wall, and then left at a signpost "Airton ½".

Follow the line indicated by the signpost, downhill. At a farm building, turn right as indicated by a "footpath" sign, to a stile with yellow arrow. Keep left towards a wall, then right, to continue over more stiles. As the wall turns away to the left, carry straight on across a meadow to the angle formed by two walls ahead, go over a stile in the field corner, and bear right towards the modern agricultural buildings at Scosthrop, entering by a farm gate to the right.

Go through the complex, left at a concrete roadway, then left again at the public road. On reaching the main road, turn right for the village green. At the green, turn left past the "squatter house", noting what appear to be the support posts for a set of stocks, and descend towards the river, passing the Friends Meeting House and a cottage dated 1696 on the way. There are former mill buildings of impressive size by the bridge.

Cross and turn left at once to follow one of the more docile sections of the great Pennine Way footpath. The Way makes a splendid return route as far as Hanlith, entirely pleasant and without any complication whatsoever, bridges, stiles, and signposts all being obvious, with the river always close at hand.

"Level" walkers will leave the Pennine Way at the beautiful bridge below Hanlith Hall, as it climbs the valley side before turning towards Malham. Cross the minor road into a surfaced lane opposite, signposted "riverside walk to Malham". At Scalegill Mill the path passes to the rear of the buildings. Beyond the mill, the size and construction of the mill pond and the water supply leat is evidence of the former importance of the mill. The weir and water intake from the river are a considerable distance upstream.

The National Park information centre is soon in view and the path is always obvious on the ground as it heads for the road and the car park.

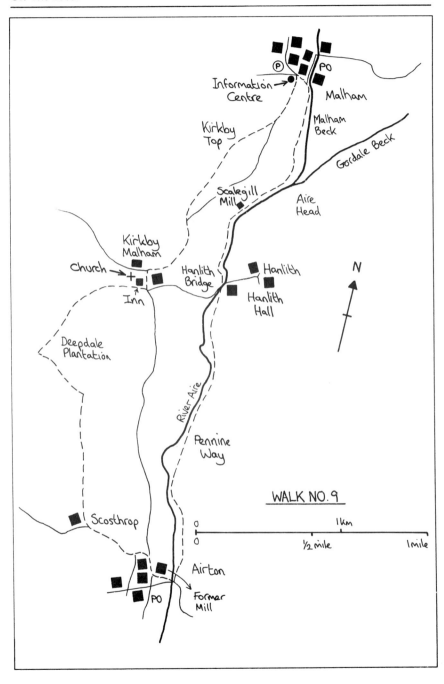

Janet's Foss waterfall

10

Malham, Janet's Foss & Gordale Scar

Length: 3 miles

Rise and Fall: 200 feet, mainly on the return by the minor road.

Underfoot: First rate footpaths and minor road.

Car Parking: Pay and display car park at entrance to Malham village. Grid reference: 900627.

Map: Ordnance Survey Outdoor Leisure No. 10 Yorkshire Dales, Southern area. 1 : 25000.

Description

Malham is claimed to be the most visited centre in the whole of the Yorkshire Dales National Park, a figure of 500,000 visitors per annum being estimated. It is certainly at the heart of the most spectacular Dales limestone scenery, Malham Cove and Gordale Scar both being close at hand. A high proportion of the visitors are walkers – the Pennine Way passes through and the whole area is criss-crossed by footpaths. Unfortunately for "level" walkers, this rugged countryside rises and falls steeply; the steps beside Malham Cove are a good example of the effort needed even on very popular routes.

This easy little walk has been included to provide a view of the magnificent crags and waterfalls at Gordale Scar, coupled with Janet's Foss, and all on a very good surface underfoot. The return along the road, with its rise of about 130 feet, is recommended for its wider, different, views, but to return along the excellent Janet's Foss footpath avoids the rise and would be acceptable to most walkers.

Janet's Foss is a waterfall of more than usual geological interest, having a screen of tufa over the underlying rock. There is also a local legend about the fairy who lived in the adjacent cave. It is a delectable spot on a fine day, when bathing in the pool might well attract at least the younger members of a party. The surrounding woodland and other vegetation is notably rich.

Malham is well provided with inns, cafes, shops, information centre, and public conveniences.

Route

From the car park pass the National Park Information Centre, turn left towards the village and, in 60 yards, turn right over a footbridge, then right again. Follow the footpath signposted "Pennine Way, Janet's Foss 1¼m. Gordale Scar 1½m." The well-made track runs alongside Malham Beck to a ladder stile. At a kissing gate turn left to leave the Pennine Way by a "footpath Janet's Foss" signpost.

The track onward is quite unmistakeable, so popular that it has twin kissing gates and ladder stiles as it follows the line of the Gordale Beck, with improved farmland on the left and poor, badly drained, land on the right. The Malham Tarn Estate (National Trust) woodland is entered and the surroundings become more glen-like as the waterfall is approached, the path being more up and down and with a few tree roots to disturb its otherwise even surface.

Gordale Scar

By the waterfall is certainly a place to linger unless, of course, a large and noisy school field study party has taken possession of the site. An information board provides a useful brief description.

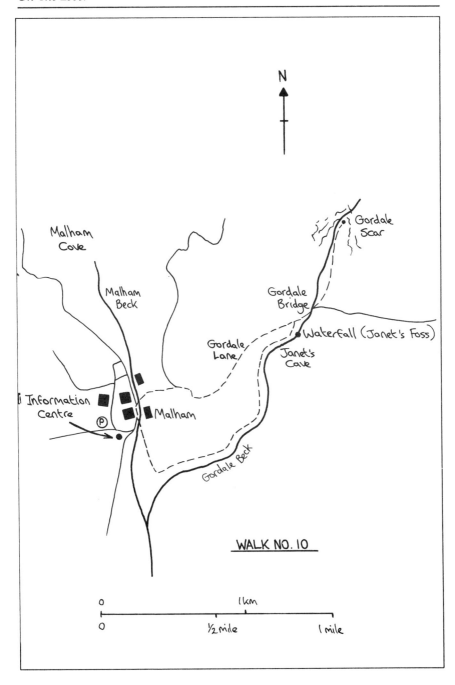

N

Malham
Cove

Malham
Beck

Gordale
Scar

Gordale
Bridge

Gordale
Lane

Waterfall (Janet's Foss)

Janet's
Cave

Information
Centre

ⓟ

Malham

Gordale Beck

WALK NO. 10

0
|——————————————————————|
0   ½ mile   1 mile

1 km

Leave the Foss by a rising path to the left, for a few yards on solid rock, to reach the minor road. Turn right to Gordale Bridge which has superseded the rather nicer old bridge. The broad, easy, track to Gordale Scar is to the left, again with an information board. There is no avoiding an out-and-back walk for the quarter of a mile to the Scar, but it really is worth it: cliffs more than 160 feet high, only 30 feet apart at the base, and plunging waterfalls. The path does, in fact, continue up the gorge but there is some serious scrambling involved.

To return to Malham along the road necessitates a climb of 130 feet at a maximum gradient of 1 in 6. If this does not appeal, retrace your steps past the Foss. The road is exceptionally quiet and does have the advantage of long views as it heads directly back to the village, passing the youth hostel and the Lister's Arms Hotel before turning left in the village to pass the Buck Arms and return to the car park.

Malham village

II

Malham Tarn Circular

Length: 3 miles

Rise and Fall: 170 feet, all at gentle gradients.

Underfoot: About half on very minor roads, half on broad, easy, tracks.

Car Parking: Close to the point where the Malham Beck crosses the road below the Tarn is a rough surfaced parking area. Grid reference: 895658.

Map: Ordnance Survey Outdoor Leisure No. 10, Yorkshire Dales, Southern area. 1 : 25000

Description

Malham Tarn, second largest natural lake in Yorkshire, is included within the 4200 acre Malham Tarn Estate, owned by the National Trust. The lake lies at more than 1200 feet above sea level and is of international nature conservation importance. Although surrounded by limestone countryside, the water sits in a saucer-shaped basin of much older Silurian period rock, with a natural dam of material dumped by glaciers during the ice age. The unusual combination of conditions has resulted in the presence of many rare plants and much of the area is a nature reserve managed by the Field Studies Council and the National Trust. Access to the reserve is by permit only.

Tarn House was built in the late 18th century as a shooting lodge, used by Lord Ribblesdale. It was later used as a country house and was visited by many eminent Victorians, including Charles Darwin and Charles Kingsley. Kingsley was inspired by the area to write the "Water Babies" story. The house is now used as a field studies centre. Wildlife around Malham Tarn is also important: hides have been constructed from which mallard, coot, great crested grebe, and other waterfowl can be observed.

Route

From the car park walk to the road and turn right, crossing Malham Beck. Continue past Low Trenhouse, dated 1907 but looking older. Prominent away to the left of the road is the base of a chimney stack which served a former lead smelt mill later converted to process calamine, a zinc ore.

At a road junction turn right, pass High Trenhouse, now converted into a "Centre for Management Creativity" and keep right at another junction, signposted "Arncliffe". In about 200 yards, go through a gate on the right to follow a straight, stony-surfaced, lane. At a surfaced roadway, turn right.

The roadway loses its surface, the Pennine Way joins from the left, and the grounds of Tarn House are entered. The way rises steadily through woodland, mostly early 19th century plantation, providing shelter for the House. There is a mixture of broad leaved species, including the non-native sycamore, with some larch and scots pine. The House, beautifully sited above the lake, is reached through a rock cutting.

The way passes behind the buildings and continues downhill, over a stile, emerging into open country by the lake shore. After a farm gate, as the Pennine Way bends left, fork right towards the edge of a plantation, and then left to aim straight for the car park. The route is well-marked on the ground.

Farm building at Malham Tarn

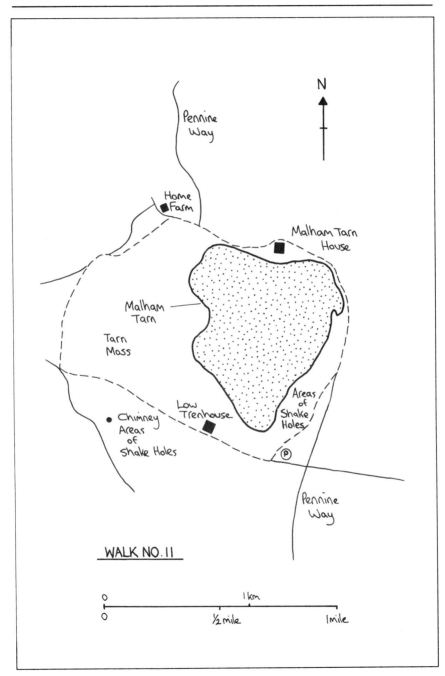

N

Pennine
Way

Home
Farm

Malham Tarn
House

Malham
Tarn

Tarn
Moss

Low
Trenhouse

Areas
of
Shake
Holes

• Chimney
Areas
of
Shake Holes

Ⓟ

Pennine
Way

WALK NO. 11

0   1 km
0   ½ mile   1 mile

12

Ribblesdale: Settle & Stainforth

Length: 6 miles

Rise and Fall: approximately 470 feet. The main ascent is the steep pull of about 180 feet out of Langcliffe (for which an alternative is available). The lane rising from the bridge at Stainforth is also quite steep, but the rise is less than 100 feet.

Underfoot: Some road, otherwise good field paths and lanes. The final descent into Settle has a roughish stony section.

Car Parking: Pay and display in Settle town. Grid reference: 819638.

Map: Ordnance Survey Outdoor Leisure No. 2 Yorkshire Dales, Western area. 1 : 25000.

Description

Settle has been described as the "capital" of upper Craven, a bustling little town with its market charter granted by King Henry III in 1248. Market day is Tuesday. There are good buildings of the 17th – 19th centuries, including

Settle – "The Folly"

the "Folly" in the High Street, built in 1679 by Thomas Preston, a man whose ambitions exceeded his purse to the extent that he was unable to finish the construction. All normal town facilities are to be found in Settle; there is a particularly good choice of refreshments around the Market Place.

The town is separated from its western suburb and from Giggleswick beyond by the great embankment of the Settle and Carlisle railway, built during the 1870s when the Midland Railway Company, determined to have its totally independent share of the Scottish trade, forged this heroic route through the Pennines. In recent decades this line has remained in use against all the odds and against several attempts by British Rail to do away with it. The service has been progressively downgraded, but the support from powerful groups, including many local people, should safeguard its retention for the foreseeable future.

The high moors and limestone scarps or "scars", so typical of the Craven part of the Dales, are cut by the broad swathe of the River Ribble as it flows south before turning to the west to reach the Irish Sea near Preston. Behind Settle, to the east, Attermire Scar has caves which have yielded finds of historical importance.

Stainforth and Langcliffe are pleasant villages, the former being close to the popular waterfall of Stainforth Force and having both an inn and an official picnic area.

The River Ribble above Settle

Route

From the car park turn left, under the railway, and walk along the main road towards the river. Cross the bridge, from which a former mill building, now converted into apartments, and its weir with fish ladder, can be seen. Before the school buildings turn right at a signpost "Stackhouse". The track has a fence on the left and a wall on the right as it heads for the river. On reaching the bank, go over a stile to follow a grassy track across a wide meadow, with mill buildings and chimney ahead. The Ribble valley is broad and gentle, but the harsher uplands with their limestone scars are never out of sight.

There is a close view of the very mixed buildings of the mill as the track passes along the steep bank behind, well-wooded with ash, that grand tree of the Dales, dominant. There are stiles to cross before the path angles left towards a minor road, joined at yet another stile.

Turn right along the road, keeping right where a lesser road enters the hamlet of Stackhouse. Immediately past a detached house turn right into an unsurfaced lane signposted "footpath Locks ¼m." A large weir with fish ladder and footbridge add interest at this point where water is taken from the river to the mill. Turn left over a stile signposted "Stainforth Bridge 1.5m".

The path is now quite delightful, along the edge of the river, crossing the limestone walls at frequent intervals by a variety of stiles, and with a close view of the not particularly attractive back of another mill. There is some muddy, cattle-trodden, ground hereabouts. After a gap in a wall, keep right to stay close by the river. There is one steep little bank to climb as the path rises above the river.

By a gate giving access to a static caravan site, keep right to head for a ladder stile and Stainforth Force, where the Ribble cascades down rocky steps like a mini Aysgarth, an ideal picnic site.

Continue over the bridge and follow the lane steeply uphill to the main road, crossing the railway on the way. Turn right towards Stainforth, a visit to the village needing a diversion to the left. The road is followed for a short distance, with Stainforth Scar close and impressive on the left. Before the entrance to the youth hostel, as the road dips to the right, turn left at a signpost "Langcliffe". The route is not well-marked on the ground, but follow the line indicated by the signpost across a big field. The wall to the right is the boundary with the railway, which has just emerged from a small tunnel at this point. Just over a rise a ladder stile can be seen on the wall ahead, reached by crossing a small stream. The route remains about the same distance from the wall on the right, before dipping sharply to the right by

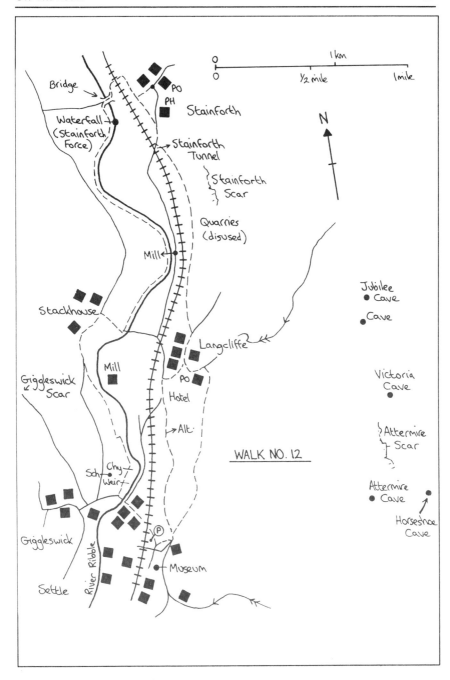

WALK NO. 12

the side of a stone construction, presumably part of the former quarries ahead and to the left.

After a stile there is another dip, steps, a plank bridge, and a great long stone-built industrial building, again obviously an interesting relic of the disused quarries. At the far end of this structure is a Craven District Council depot yard. Bear right at a cottage to a "footpath" sign with yellow arrows, right by the side of the railway. Continue to a rudimentary flight of steps, cross the road, and follow the sign to "Langcliffe ¾", rising gently. There is a stile, then a grassy meadow. Head for a break in a wall, under a hawthorn, and along the top of a bank. The track continues to rise to a ladder stile, then a stile over a fence, before levelling out and continuing by further ladder stiles to reach a lane leading into Langcliffe village.

At a junction keep left towards the church, turn left up the road and, in 60 yards, fork right at a farm gate with a signpost "B.W. Settle ¾". There is now a steep rise which continues to just above the first visible cross wall ahead; including the height already gained in the village, the total ascent is about 180 feet.

[If this is daunting, there is an alternative. Turn right through Langcliffe to rejoin the valley road, turning left towards Settle. At a junction in less than 300 yards go left along a minor road to Townhead]

As the angle of the wall is reached, turn right; the track soon levels out. The views across the broad expanse of Ribblesdale and over the rooftops of Langthwaite are fair compensation for the uphill slog. The way proceeds by a gate, and a ladder stile, the field walls converging to form a broad, grassy, lane heading towards Settle, now well seen below, with the railway embankment emphasising the division between the old part of the town and its western suburb.

There is a stony surface underfoot before a surfaced road is reached. Go straight on into Townhead, with its lovely old cottages, and bear right at a junction to reach the Market Place, then right again to return to the car park.

13

Clapham & Austwick

Length: 4 miles

Rise and Fall: about 370 feet, most of which is included in the initial climb from Clapham along Thwaite Lane at a moderately steep gradient. Thereafter, the lane and the return footpath are generally level with very minor rises and falls.

Underfoot: Apart from the odd muddy section, Thwaites Lane is very good, while the return footpath with its close-cropped grass is a joy to walk.

Car Parking: As for Walk 14.

Map: Ordnance Survey Outdoor Leisure No. 2 Yorkshire Dales, Western area. 1 : 25000

Description

Clapham is described in walk 14. This modest circuit visits another good village, Austwick, using an old lane with wide open views of the scarred limestone country so typical of the Craven district, the return being along a delightful field path.

New Inn, Clapham

Austwick has an attractive area around the green, with a "cross" and some genuinely old buildings, with the Moorcock Inn prominent. The post office/store is nearby.

Route

Leave the car park by the entrance and turn right, soon reaching the church. Take the signposted bridleway on the right which becomes Thwaites Lane, climbing steadily to its junction with Long Lane and a signpost "Austwick 1½". Carry straight on. The summit of Ingleborough can be seen behind to the left, 3½ miles away, with Robin Proctor's Scar and Nappa Scars much closer on the left, roughly parallel with the lane.

Route finding is hardly required as the lane continues across the semi-moorland, with only the odd plantation of trees to break the wind which sweeps across this area. 350 yards after passing the oddly named Long Tram Plantation there is a ladder stile on the right with a right of way to Austwick which cuts off a corner. However, there is no clear path on the ground and it costs little in distance to continue along the lane to a junction, to turn right, and to reach Austwick ("Eastern settlement") at Town Head, along the minor surfaced road.

Turn right at a more important road. The village is long, with a linear shape and some good old stone buildings, a few dating from the 17th century. Look out for decorated lintels. The prettiest area is by the small green, where the "cross" has been restored. Turn right at the road junction by the church and take the stile over the wall on the right in 200 yards, signposted "Clapham 2 miles". It may be of comfort to know that two miles is an over-estimate of the remaining distance!

The path rises up the meadow and then levels off before continuing by a ladder stile with a yellow marker and aiming for the upper side of a small copse. Look at the terracing of this field, which shows evidence of an ancient cultivation system. The site of a "settlement"is passed on the left, 300 yards after the copse. The path continues over good grass, via ladder stiles and kissing gates, always clear on the ground, all the way to Clapham. The elevation is sufficient to give long views over the dale, basically the valley of the River Wenning, which can be fully enjoyed on a footpath which provides such easy walking.

Clapham is reached at a kissing gate at the muddy approach to a farm. Go straight ahead towards a concreted area, guided by "footpath" signs, take a kissing gate on the right, and return over a stile to the car park.

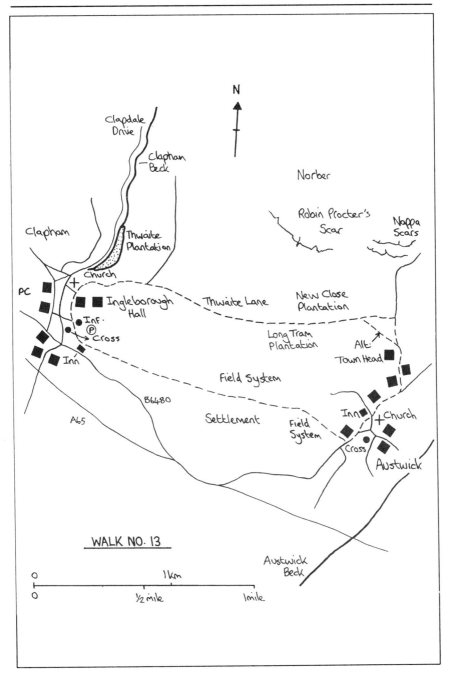

Clapdale
Drive

Claphan
Beck

N

Norber

Robin Procter's
Scar

Nappa
Scars

Clapham

Thwaite
Plantation

Church

PC

Ingleborough
Hall

Thwaite Lane

New Close
Plantation

Inf.
Ⓟ
Cross

Long Tram
Plantation

Alt.
Town Head

Inn

Field System

B6480

A65

Settlement

Field
System

Inn

Church

Cross

Austwick

WALK NO. 13

0   1 Km
0
        ½ mile   1 mile

Austwick
Beck

14

Clapham & The Ingleborough Estate

Length: 3 miles

Rise and Fall: 370 feet, mostly at easy gradients.

Underfoot: Clapdale Drive, Long Lane, and Thwaite Lane are excellent. The field after the bridge is likely to be rough and muddy.

Car Parking: Pay and display car park in Clapham village. Grid reference: 746693.

Map: Ordnance Survey Outdoor Leisure No. 2 Yorkshire Dales, Western area. 1 : 25000

Description

Clapham is without doubt one of the nicest villages in the Yorkshire Dales. Happily by-passed by the busy A65 main road, it is a popular centre for Dales walkers, Ingleborough Cave, Gaping Gill, and the summit of Ingleborough all being within reach. Less ambitious walkers can sample the countryside of this dominantly limestone part of the Craven district by the circuit, largely within the Ingleborough Estate, described below, or by the following walk, Clapham and Austwick. For a longer expedition, the two can readily be combined by following this route as far as the junction with Thwaite Lane and then turning left to head for Austwick. By the car park in Clapham are National Park Information Centre, public conveniences, and cafe; the post office/stores is over the bridge.

Route

At the car park exit turn right and then cross the Clapham Beck by a delightful old footbridge, turning right to head for "Ingleborough Cave". After the road turns left, go right for "Estate Trail to Ingleborough Cave", being prepared to pay 20p for the privilege of passing along this trail, a wide easy trackway, climbing a little steeply at first, but soon easing to a very reasonable gradient. There is a waterfall below on the right and the ornamental lake is reached in a short distance. There is a wide variety in the surrounding woodland and undergrowth, hardly surprising as much of it was collected and planted by Reg Farrer (1880-1920) a widely travelled botanist and a member of the family which has owned the estate for many years. The same family is still in control of its management.

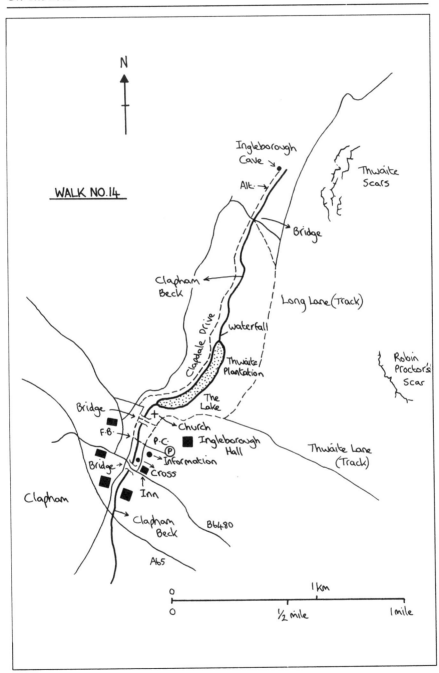

There are seats at frequent intervals, from which the delightful, glen-like, scenery can be admired. The woodland is left at a kissing gate, with Ingleborough Cave only 400 yards further along the same track. This cave is open to visitors and would obviously combine very well with this comparatively short walk.

After the kissing gate the circuit continues by descending to the footbridge, crossing the beck, and ascending across the field beyond. The O.S. map shows the right of way as keeping close to the wall on the left, giving a steep and direct route to Long Lane. On the ground, however, it does appear that most walkers angle well to the right, much reducing the gradient (and saving an extra 80 feet or so of ascent). Either way, this cattle-churned field will be muddy. The angled route, clear on the ground, passes through a gap in a wall then aims for the far corner of the next field, where a small gate gives access to the lane.

Turn right to follow the broad stony lane; the exposed rocks of Thwaite Scars are above to the left. Thwaite Lane is joined after a dip and a rise. Turn right to return downhill to Clapham, reaching the village by the side of the parish church, largely rebuilt in the 19th century, and continue to the car park.

Ancient footbridge, Clapham

15

Ingleton and its waterfalls

Length: short walk, 2¼ miles; circuit, 3½ miles.

Rise and Fall: short walk, 140 feet; circuit, 425 feet.

Underfoot: For the short walk, the track as far as the footbridge is first-rate; thereafter it becomes more varied, clinging to the side of the valley of the River Doe, aided by flights of steps. For the circuit, Oddies Lane, on the line of a Roman road, makes a pleasant return to Ingleton.

Car Parking: Pay and display car park on the site of the former railway station in Ingleton, well-signposted. Grid reference: 695730

Map: Ordnance Survey Outdoor Leisure No. 2 Yorkshire Dales, Western area. 1 : 25000

Description

Although situated very much on the western fringe of the Yorkshire Dales National Park, Ingleton is very close indeed to the two highest mountains, Whernside and Ingleborough. It follows that the village is an important centre for hill walkers and, because of the geology, is also well-situated for caving enthusiasts. Despite appearances from the main road and from the road over the hills to Hawes, the village centre is attractive and is well-provided with inns, cafes, shops, and a youth hostel. The car park has a tourist information centre and public conveniences.

The dominant feature is the fine viaduct which carried the long defunct Clapham to Low Gill railway line over the river valley. The small rivers Doe and Wiss tumble down rocky valleys to meet in Ingleton, then becoming the River Greta. These two valleys give the village a superb local environment and its reputation as the village of waterfalls. The "Waterfalls Walk" is well-signposted and is a very popular circuit visiting the Pecca Falls, Thornton Falls, Beezley Falls, and Snow Falls. The walk is rather more than four miles long and has a great deal of rise and fall as the riverside path, with many flights of steps, ascends the valley of the Wiss, reaches nearly 1100 feet, crosses the intermediate country by Twisleton Hall, and then descends the valley of the Doe. It is not always easy underfoot.

The present walk is an easy stroll as far as the rocky riverside area, the footbridge, and the Snow Falls. To return from here to Ingleton by the same route would be entirely pleasant. However, for a longer walk, and to complete a circuit, the rise and fall between Snow Falls and Beezley Falls has been minimized; the elevated return from Beezleys Farm has views to Ingleborough.

Beezley Falls, Ingleton

Route

From the car park there is a flight of steps down to the road. Turn right, to the village centre, keeping to the right of St Mary's church – the tower and the font are both Norman. At the Square go straight across, opposite the National Westminster bank, and follow Thacking Lane out of the built-up area. The valley of the River Doe is below to the left as the surfaced lane rises to end at a gate.

Continue along the path, passing a disused quarry, before an uphill stretch leads to an old kissing gate. Here a sign states that (high) charges are made for using the Waterfall Walk, payment being made at the exit. There was no evidence of request for payment either here or at Beezleys, where the Waterfall Walk route is left. The path now goes gently downhill to an attractive riverside area with rapids, rock faces and a disused quarry. A few steps and a fenced path along the side of a ravine lead to the footbridge. Two

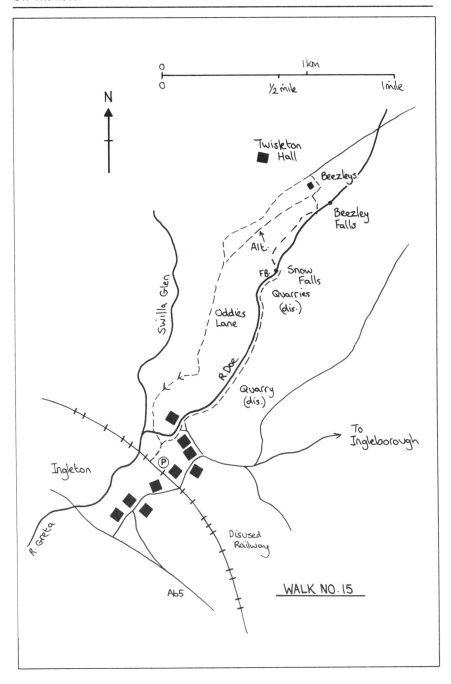

WALK NO. 15

further flights of steps reach the Snow Falls, which make a satisfying termination of the short out and back walk.

To complete the circuit, ascend a longer flight of steps and, at the top, fork left along a minor path towards a farm gate. Bend right over a sleeper bridge before the gate and continue close to the fence/wall, a path being just about evident as it skirts around the heads of two small but deep tributary valleys.

The main path is rejoined by a kissing gate close to the Beezley Falls. After viewing the falls, proceed to Beezley farmstead. To the left before the buildings are the starts of two rights of way across the farmland/caravan site. Neither is signposted or visible on the ground, but it is possible to follow the approximate line of the upper route before joining the public road half a mile nearer to Ingleton. If this does not appeal go past the farm and join the old Roman road, Oddies Lane, turning left. This little used lane makes a perfectly acceptable return route to Ingleton. At the foot of the lane, turn left over the bridge to the village centre.

16

Ingleton & Chapel le Dale

Length: 5 miles

Rise and Fall: approximately 400 feet, most being in the initial ascent from Chapel le Dale to Ellerbeck.

Underfoot: A high proportion of farm roadways, good field paths and less than half a mile of public road. Of particular note is that, on the whole circuit, there is not a single stile which has to be negotiated.

Car Parking: Space for a few cars close to the church at Chapel le Dale. Grid reference: 738772.

Map: Ordnance Survey Outdoor Leisure No. 2 Yorkshire Dales, Western area. 1 : 25000

Description

Above Ingleton, the two great mountain masses of Whernside and Ingleborough dominate a wild area of high ground. This is classic limestone country with all the expected features: caves, pot holes, dry stream beds, underground water, and shake holes. This area will be familiar to many from school geography lessons; having pored over a section of the old one-inch O.S. map, – "given its high rainfall, why are there no continuing streams draining the flanks of Ingleborough, and why do so many small streams appear to terminate high on the mountain?"

In the valley between the two great mountains trees are very few indeed, making the wooded hamlet of Chapel le Dale, snug in its sheltering hollow, particularly attractive. Arguably, the upland scenery would be better without the so very obviously artificial conifer plantation on West Moss.

A dominant feature of the walk is the Ribblehead viaduct. Of all the fine engineering features of the Settle and Carlisle railway, this viaduct has come to epitomise the determination and the hardship involved in building a railway across such wild and difficult country. The tiny 17th century chapel at Chapel le Dale is particularly associated with those who died during construction in the 1870s. In modern times, the deterioration of the structure of the viaduct was a fundamental part of British Rail's case in their efforts to close the line.

Route

Turn right, uphill, by the church, along a surfaced lane designated as a bridleway, soon passing an impressive hole on the right. Go straight on at a junction, signposted "Ellerbeck", still climbing steadily. There is a piece of modern sculpture by the wayside before the 1607 farmhouse of Gill Head is reached. Here, the Chapel le Dale estate has planted a variety of trees during the past 30 years, many of which are now well-grown.

Above this area the track emerges into open country, with a great deal of exposed limestone, as it heads for Ellerbeck Farm, below the broad flank of Whernside. There is a first view of the viaduct away to the right. At a ford the track bends right, signposted "Deepdale 7¾", passes through Ellerbeck Farm, then loses its surface as it continues on the far side as an attractive bridleway, accompanied by a low scarp, to Bruntscar.

The old buildings, including a farm house dated 1689, are rather decrepit. [Just after the farm there is a right turn, signposted "Hill Inn" which provides a short return route to Chapel le Dale]. Continue straight on and, as the path bends left to climb Whernside, take a little gate ahead, signposted "Winterscales 1¼". The path is clear on the grass as it heads for Broadrake, the next farm, passing across the front of the buildings. [There is another opportunity to turn right here should you wish to shorten the walk]

St Leonard's church, Chapel le Dale

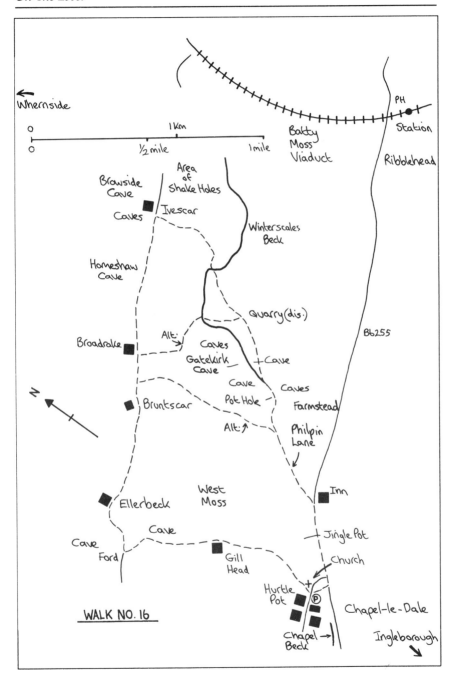

Whernside

1 Km
½ mile   1 mile

PH
Station
Batty
Moss
Viaduct
Ribblehead

Area
of
Shake Holes

Browside
Cave

Caves   Ivescar

Winterscales
Beck

Homeshaw
Cave

Quarry (dis.)

B6255

Broadrake

Alt:

Caves
Gatekirk
Cave   + Cave

Cave   Caves
Pot Hole   Farmstead

Brunkscar

Philpin
Lane

Alt:↗

West
Moss   Inn

Ellerbeck

Cave   Jingle Pot

Cave   Church
Ford   Gill
Head

Hurtle
Pot   P   Chapel-le-Dale

WALK NO. 16   Chapel →
Beck   Ingleborough

There are small gates at each cross wall as the path heads for an obvious house. Next is Ivescar Farm, which has an area with caves behind to the left. Here our route turns right, along the farm access roadway. The land is a mixture of totally uncultivated rough grazing with better, brighter, green areas which generations of farmers have struggled to maintain as "improved" land for the benefit of their cattle and sheep. Carry on to cross the bridge over the dry Winterscales Beck, in about 400 yards further reaching a cattle grid.

As the roadway bends left, uphill, take a just visible path on the right, rising to a small gate in the angle of two walls. Follow a grassy path by the wall and, as the wall turns away, keep straight on, downhill, to Winterscales Beck and an area so typical of this limestone country: a disappearing stream; a large hole in the ground; the sound of tumbling water; caves, and a pot hole.

Cross the stream bed to a farm gate and ladder stile. Carry on to a small gate but, as the sunken lane beyond is wet and badly overgrown, keep just right until a farm gate is reached. Join the sunken lane here, reaching a surfaced lane in a few yards, and turn left to rise a little to the public road close to the isolated Old Hill Inn. Turn right to return downhill to Chapel le Dale.

Gill Head, Chapel le Dale

17

Sedbergh Circular

Length: 5 miles

Rise and Fall: Almost 500 feet, well-distributed and without severe gradients.

Underfoot: A total mixture, with road (1 mile), excellent riverside footpath, and field paths. Some of the field paths are indistinct on the ground, with several areas likely to be muddy.

Car Parking: Free public car park (Loftus Hill) on the Dent road in Sedbergh. Grid reference: 657920.

Map: Ordnance Survey Outdoor Leisure no. 2 Yorkshire Dales, Western area. 1 : 25000

Description

Sedbergh is a thriving little market town of some charm, although the cobbled surface which enhances the appearance of the main street is likely to be replaced in the near future. Installed a few years ago as an "olde worlde" visual enhancement, it has proved to be unpopular with the towns-folk.

The town sits close by the foot of the shapely Howgill Fells, quite a favourite of the late A. Wainwright. Early prosperity was linked with the wool trade – the period from the late 17th to early 18th centuries was a particularly prosperous time, and many fine yeomen's ("statesmen's") houses were built during this period in and around Sedbergh. Most of these houses are still evident.

The famous Sedbergh public school was founded as a chantry school in 1552 and by the beginning of the 18th century it was claimed to be the most prominent school in the north of England. The extensive playing fields are a dominant feature in Sedbergh.

Together with the adjacent Garsdale and Dentdale, in 1974 Sedbergh suffered the fate of transfer from its native Yorkshire into the newly created county of Cumbria, resulting in the very odd situation of being within the Yorkshire Dales National Park but some miles outside Yorkshire. There is a National Park Information Centre.

The countryside traversed by this walk is a mixture of gentle riverside and upland farming, with a little bit of moorland added for good measure. The views to the Howgill Fells are superb.

Street scene, Sedbergh

Route

Turn right from the car park and then right again to walk either along the main street or the parallel Back Lane. As the two streets come together, turn right at a surfaced lane signposted "Settlebeck or Milnthrop". The surface is soon lost; at the bottom of the slope go straight on through a kissing gate to take a footpath rising past the entrance to Winder House.

Go through another kissing gate and straight on to a stile. Choose the middle of the three possible routes to descend across a field towards the river, over a stile in the fence at the bottom, and alongside a waterway which has every appearance of being a mill leat. Cross a footbridge, go over a stile, and keep left along a causeway-like path beside the River Rawthey.

On reaching a main road, bear left, turn right along the road for a few yards, and then left down concrete steps to continue the riverside path. With the occasional stile, footbridge and a flight of repaired steps, this excellent path continues as far as Straight Bridge. Leave the river here, cross the road bridge, and turn right into a surfaced lane signposted "Dowbiggin". The lane rises slightly through pleasantly pastoral countryside, passing Dowbiggin Foot.

Turn right at Broad Yeat Barn to take a signposted footpath to Hallbank. Immediately after the last building, and before a stream, the path bears right and then left at a farm gate, crosses a muddy area and then rises along the edge of a field before crossing diagonally to the right, making for the angle at the junction of two fences. Keep roughly the same line, downhill, with the buildings of Hallbank on a rise, ahead and right of the required line. Descend to the Clough River, turn left on joining the riverside path, and make for a stile and footbridge.

Cross the river by the bridge and rise to the Garsdale road, turning left to follow the road uphill, accompanied by a gurgling stream, to Frostrow Methodist Chapel. Turn right just after the Chapel at a signpost "Side Farm", cross the stream by a footbridge, bend right to a farm gate, and proceed past Branthwaites Lodge. After the lodge there is a footpath sign at a farm gate, pointing the way over some fencing without a stile.

Stride over the fence, keep it close on the right, bending left as a wall is reached, to a stile in the top corner of the field. Go over the stile and continue towards an isolated farm building. Turn left at the end of the wall and struggle across an unpleasantly muddy area before bearing right to a farm gate followed by a second gate in 30 yards. A deep rutted farm vehicle track leads directly to Side Farm.

Go through the farm and exit by the farm access roadway. Pass High

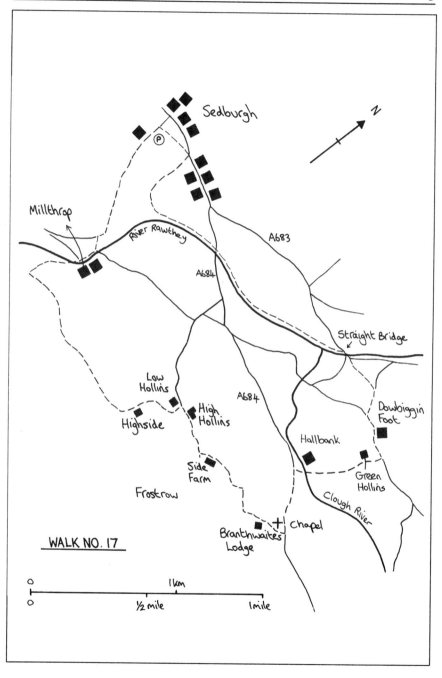

Sedburgh

N

Millthrop

River Rawthey

A683

A684

Straight Bridge

Low Hollins

High Hollins

Highside

A684

Dowbiggin Foot

Side Farm

Hallbank

Green Hollins

Frostrow

Clough River

WALK NO. 17

Branthwaites Lodge

Chapel

1 km

½ mile   1 mile

Hollins, but at Low Hollins turn left into a narrow lane climbing fairly steeply to a gate with a notice giving advice about a footpath. Go right to stay with the farm track leading directly to Highside. Pass to the right of the farm and go straight ahead up the bank at the rear. The stile here has been obstructed but there is a farm gate close on the left. Go through the farm gate at the top corner of the bank, bending right along the wall to reach moorland.

Among the rushes there is a discernable path. As this forks, keep right, still close to the wall. As the wall ends, the track is visible on the slope ahead. As the track continues across the moor, the views to the Howgills, above Sedbergh town, are magnificent. Aim for the depression between the main moor top, Long Rigg, and the slight mound to the right. As the watershed is reached, boggy ground must be crossed, after which the path becomes better defined, heading downhill to the right of small walled fields which have been wrested from the harsh moorside.

A broad, stony, track, once again part of the Dales Way continuous footpath, is reached just after passing a ruin; turn right to descend to Millthrop, an old hamlet with a long row of attractive cottages. Go along the street, then turn left to reach the Sedbergh to Dent road. Turn right, cross the bridge over the River Rawthey, and return along the road to the car park.

Bridge over the River Rawthey

18

Dentdale: Dent & Gawthrop

Length: 4¼ miles (shorter option 2¼ miles)

Rise and Fall: about 230 feet. Almost all the ascent is close to the start of the walk and the gradients are modest.

Underfoot: Generally good assortment of farm tracks, footpaths, and meadows. Almost one mile on very quiet lane.

Car Parking: Pay and Display car park in Dent town. Grid reference: 704871.

Map: Ordnance Survey Outdoor Leisure No. 2 Yorkshire Dales, Western area: 1 : 25000

Description

This walk gives another opportunity to admire the attractive farming coun-try of Dentdale, with old farmsteads strung along both sides of the valley, presumably at the level at which reliable sources of spring water could be obtained both in summer and in winter. The going is quite varied, including farm tracks, barely discernible field paths, some minor road, and a good

Dentdale from Gawthrop

length of the Dales Way. The initial rise to and beyond Mill Beck Farm is
reasonable and the reward, in the extent of the views, makes the effort
worthwhile. As mentioned in the description to Walk 19, Dent town is full
of interest.

Cottage at Gawthrop

Route

Leave the car park by the road entrance, turn right past the old post office
and, in just over 100 yards, turn left at a signpost "Gawthrop ¾ mile". Go
through the farm yard, passing a dairy shop, turn right and pass through a
farm gate marked " camping and caravan entrance only", and bear left to a
wall with a signpost. Go over the stile ahead and bear left, uphill, to proceed
through the yard of Millbeck Farm. Continue over a stile on the right, behind
a farm building, cross two small fields, to ascend a steep but short farm access
road.

Turn right to follow yellow arrows through the farm complex and a finger
post pointing to "Gawthrop". Another short rise reaches the summit of the
walk, with a bird's eye view of Dent town behind, somewhat blemished by
the preponderance of camping and caravan sites. Ahead, the Howgill fells

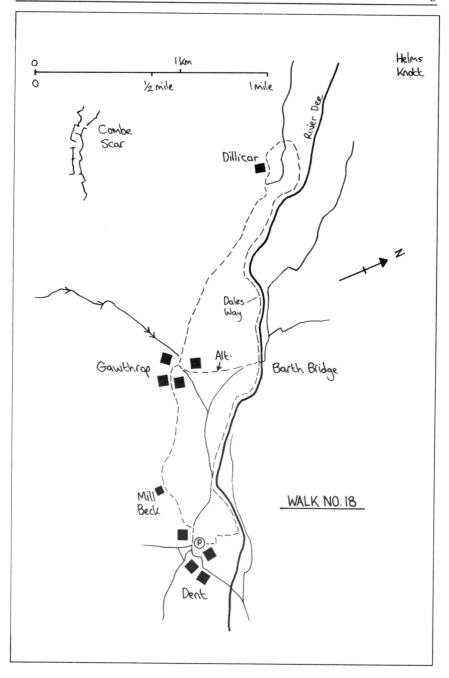

show up well in the distance, and Helms Knott is the shapely end of a nearer ridge on the far side of the dale. Closer, on the left, is the impressive amphitheatre of Combe Scar.

The track continues through a gateway in 100 yards (yellow arrow) and is easy to follow to Gawthrop. Cross the stream and, after admiring the many handsome stone houses of the hamlet, bear right to join a minor road by a seat and telephone box.

(For the short walk option turn right, downhill, and then left in 30 yards at a "footpath to Barth Bridge" sign. Follow this path down to join a road, turning left to reach Barth Bridge in 150 yards, where the main route is rejoined).

For the full circuit, turn left and walk along the road for just over three quarters of a mile. The hedgerows are full of the aromatic Ransoms (wild garlic) and blue bells. Where the road dips to the right, carry straight on along a cul de sac roadway signposted "footpath to Dillicar Farm", noteworthy for its very unfriendly (chained!) dogs. Leave the farm by a gate and angle to the right across a meadow to reach a ladder stile by the roadside. If the small ascent (or the dogs) doesn't appeal, you can stay on the road to arrive at this same point.

Cross the road, angling left to a stile with a signpost. Bear right across the field towards the River Dee, join the Dales Way, and head back towards Dent. The river bank has mature beech and other fine trees, followed by a section where ash, sycamore, and others have, many years ago, been "layered" to provide a dense barrier. The river hereabouts is placid, with deep pools attracting swallows and wagtails.

One section of the path drops a little awkwardly towards the riverbank; otherwise, the route is entirely straightforward, soon reaching Barth Bridge. Go straight across following a signpost to "Hipping ½ mile". The way is increasingly well-trodden as Dent is approached. Join the valley road, briefly, forking left in less than 100 yards at a "public footpath, Church Bridge" sign and stay close to the river bank. When a stone wall and stile are reached, turn right along an unsignposted track heading towards the car park. Turn right again through the gate opposite the waterworks building for the final uphill section through the picnic area.

The Sedgewick Stone, Dent

19

Dentdale: Dent & Cowgill

Length: 9 miles

Rise and Fall: 370 feet in total (500 feet with alternative route). Almost all the ascent is in the outward half and is well-spread with only one steep, short stretch.

Underfoot: Generally good, a varied mixture of farm footpaths and grassy meadow edges. Approximately 3½ miles on quiet lanes.

Car Parking: Pay and Display car park in Dent Town. Grid reference: 704871

Map: Ordnance Survey Outdoor Leisure No.2, Yorkshire Dales, Western area. 1: 25000.

Description

Dentdale has every appearance and attribute of a Yorkshire Dale but, like Garsdale to the north, it happens to face in the wrong direction. Instead of draining towards its native county, its waters reach the Irish Sea via the River Lune, through Cumbria and Lancashire. This unfortunate accident of geography has two results. Firstly, since 1974 and despite being part of the Yorkshire Dales National Park, the dale has belonged to Cumbria; secondly, being much less accessible from the heavily populated areas of Yorkshire than the better known east and south facing dales, and having no great tourist centres, it is a much quieter valley.

The countryside is, however, very attractive and Dent "town", as the village is known locally, is a tight knit stone-built settlement of great antiquity and character, clustered around the imposing parish church of St Andrew, despite three restorations still retaining some ancient features. Of particular note is a street fountain set in a large block of Shap granite, commemorating Dent's most famous son, Adam Sedgewick (1785-1873), the eminent geologist. The town and the dale also have a long tradition of hand knitting as a cottage industry, while for many years a hard, polishable, local limestone was quarried extensively as "Dent marble".

Varied shops, inns and cafes in the village cater for present day needs.

The present circuit is substantial for a "level" walk and offers more varied scenery than might initially be expected

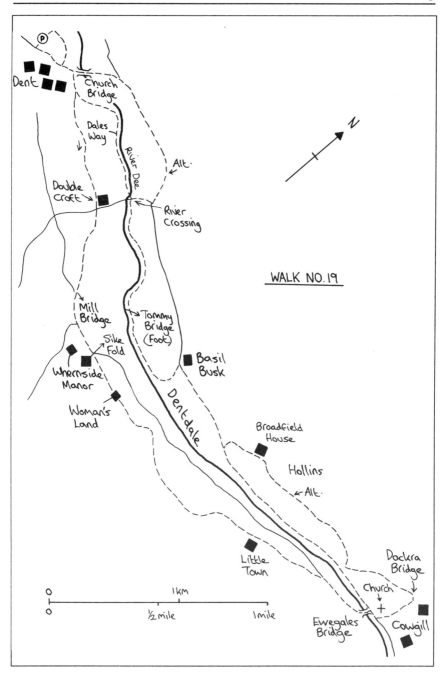

WALK NO. 19

Dent village

Route

From the car park, walk down the roadway leading from the picnic area to a farm gate marked "N.W. Water" and turn right to follow a track marked by yellow arrows to the road above Church Bridge. Immediately before the bridge, take a footpath on the right signposted to Mill Bridge, along the side of a tributary stream and over several stiles. At a junction of paths in 200 yards, ignore an obvious gate on the left and go over a stile to the right and then a plank bridge. A lightly worn track continues across the foot of several meadows, keeping close to the stream, with its banks carpeted by wild flowers. Several stiles, signs, and small bridges mark the way to Double Croft Farm, where a small gate on the right takes walkers round the back of the farm.

Proceed straight across the farm access roadway, through the gate, and keep the road close on the right, crossing lush valley bottom pastures which contrast sharply with the stark moorland rising steeply up the valley sides, bare of trees except where a few stream gullies provide enrichment of the soil and some protection from the grazing sheep. The high and wild dale-head is in view ahead with Whernside, at 2419 feet Yorkshire's highest mountain, to the right.

A more major footpath, the Dalesway, is joined at a stile; turn right here. On the left, the bed of the Deepdale Beck is dry, a reminder that we are in limestone country. The next section of the beck, with rushing water, is altogether more attractive and has a particularly rich array of vegetation. The road along the south side of the valley is soon reached at Mill Bridge, the very obvious site of a former mill complex.

Continue along the road for less than half a mile, passing Deepdale Methodist Chapel and Whernside Manor. Fifty yards after Sike Fold, turn right at a little gate with a signpost "Ewegales Bridge 2" to cross a small meadow with the short but steepest rise on the walk. Go over a ladder stile and then left to pass a farm building, the land now being altogether poorer and wilder. The elevation allows more extensive views, the Howgill Fells above Sedbergh being visible down the valley. The huge and bleak bulk of Aye Gill Pike and Rise Hill close the view to the north, with stone enclosure walls climbing all the way to the watershed. The route stays close to the wall, rather surprisingly passing through the garden and past the front door of the oddly-named "Woman's Land", leaving by a short flight of steps. Head for a ladder stile and then bear right, rising a little to follow the line of a long collapsed wall towards another ladder stile, then yellow markers around the back of Low Laithe Barn. Descend the farm roadway for a short distance and turn right at a signpost "Clint" rejoining the Dales Way at this point

The route now follows a mixture of farm roadways and well-worn footpaths passing West Clint and Clint to reach the imposing Hackergill farmhouse, dated 1866. Turn left into the access track, take a stile on the right in 50 yards and cross a meadow, looking out for a post with a marker in the next meadow, where the path is not too distinct. At the entrance to the woodland plantation the very narrow stile can be avoided by using a break in the wall 20 yards further. Enter the woodland, soon reaching Little Town in its spacious clearing. Follow the stiles around the property, back into the woodland which is very unimaginative in the planting of straight lines of single species conifers.

As the path angles gently towards the road, Dent station on the now legendary Settle and Carlisle Railway can be seen high on the moorside ahead. Along the road, Ewegales Bridge is reached, with its camping/caravan site and a welcoming seat.

Cowgill, nothing more than a farming hamlet, is accessed by crossing the bridge and turning right. Across another bridge, the 19th century church is attractively sited. Note the plaque on the bridge recording the "repere" at the charge of the West Riding in 1702. The nearest refreshments are at the Sportsman Inn, almost a mile further along the road beside the River Dee.

To return to Dent, follow the road along the north side of the River Dee for 1¾ miles. The river, with its limestone slabs, little falls and rapids, and occasional total loss of water provides interest by the side of this minor thoroughfare.

[However, if you have an aversion to walking on tarmac more than a mile can be avoided by turning left up the lane on the far side of the brook by the church, rising gradually to pass a farmstead before turning left to cross the stream by the Dockra stone bridge. Turn right, then immediately left at a stile. The route across the meadow is not worn on the ground; bear to the left to look for a stile in the far wall, after this stile keep close to a wall and maintain the same line across the next meadow, descending gradually from stile to stile. Make for the right-hand edge of the farm buildings below. At the farm, bear away to the right towards a stile and then to Spice Gill Farm. Turn right at the far end of the farm on a grass track, then left to cross a stream by a footbridge, noting a 1706 date on a building to the right. After a little gate there is a short but steep pull up a farm track, forking left as this track bends right to Allen Haw.

Pass Hollins Farm on its upper side, then a barn, and bend right to a gap on the far side of the meadow, pass the front of a small farm, bending right then left then left again round the back of more farm buildings before reaching a drive. Turn left through a gate with a faint yellow mark beside to pass in front of the substantial Broadfield House and descend the access road to return to the public road. (This variation adds about a third of a mile and 130 feet of ascent to the walk)]

Among the old farmsteads passed on the roadside, the Gibbs complex, which includes the shell of the apparently oldest hall, is particularly interesting. Opposite Basil Bush, turn left at a footpath sign "Lenny's Leap ⅛ml" and bear left across a steeply descending meadow to a footbridge over the river. Turn sharp right before the bridge to follow the riverside path for some distance passing, but not crossing, Tommy Bridge. Head for the ladder stile at the far end of the meadow. Across the river at this point are the remains of what might well be an old lime kiln.

The path stays beside the river, fringed by trees, "layered" many years ago as a stock-proof barrier, until a small gate on the left is reached. At this point the river may be crossed by the intrepid at an old ford, turning right to use the Dales Way path to return to Church Bridge and Dent. However, many of the stones used to cross the river are slippery with moss and at least one boot full of water is the likely outcome.

The more cautious will turn sharp right into a short length of sunken lane, rejoin the road, and turn left to cross Church Bridge. Obviously the direct route to the car park can be used but a small detour through the village is highly recommended.

Norman doorway at Easby Abbey

20

Richmond and Easby Abbey

Length: 2¾ miles

Rise and Fall: Very little, probably about 50 feet in total.

Underfoot: Excellent. Lanes, footpaths and the former railway line.

Car Parking: Car park by the disused railway station, also serving the town's swimming pool, signposted in town as "swimming baths". Grid reference: 175009.

Map: Ordnance Survey Pathfinder No. 609, Richmond and Leyburn. 1:25000 or Ordnance Survey Landranger No. 92, Barnard Castle and surrounding area. 1:50000.

Description

This is a very gentle, undemanding, walk from Richmond to Easby Abbey, using riverside lanes and paths for the outward journey, with the return along the disused railway line.

Space does not permit a full description of Richmond's many attractions. Suffice it to say that it is a great little town with a beautifully sited and dominant castle; there is a huge cobbled market place, sloping from end to end, a generally Georgian ambience including a restored theatre, and much more for the visitor.

Easby Abbey was founded about 1180, being of the Premonstratensian Order, and continued in use until the Dissolution. The ruins are extensive, occupying a site between the river and Easby village, situated on the hill above. The adjacent church of St Agatha, at least in part older than the Abbey, has some remarkable 13th century wall paintings in the chancel.

Richmond railway station has a well-restored facade and a new use as a horticultural sales centre. It was once the terminus of a branch line which connected with the east coast main line south of Darlington.

Route

Walk towards the town centre and cross the bridge over the River Swale, now named Mercury Bridge to commemorate the 50th anniversary of the Royal Corps of Signals at Catterick. In 40 yards turn right into a surfaced lane, then right again at a "T" junction. As the lane loses its surface, it rises a little under a canopy of trees, with the river below on the right.

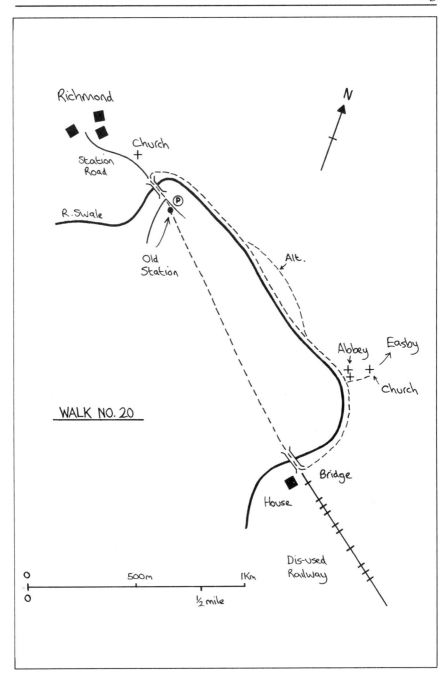

Richmond

Church

Station
Road

R. Swale

Old
Station

WALK NO. 20

Alt.

Abbey   Easby

Church

Bridge

House

Dis-used
Railway

N

0   500m   1Km
0   ½ mile

After a descent by a seat, the track forks: the path to the right stays close to the river bank, richly wooded with sycamore prominent. The path is so well-used that no route finding is necessary. A flight of steps gives a rise of 15 feet or so towards a stile. The steps may be avoided by forking left at the junction mentioned above.

The abbey ruins are now in view ahead. Continue to a stile in the right-hand corner of a field by Abbey Mill Kennels, occupying the former mill house. The abbey is in the care of English Heritage, open Tuesday – Sunday from Easter to the end of October and at weekends in winter. Before continuing the walk, don't forget the parish church!

For the return, turn right beyond the abbey, pass a small car park, and follow a stony lane, passing two dwellings, with the river close on the right. This track leads to one end of the old railway bridge. Turn right over the bridge to cross the river. Below are tempting picnic/recreation areas on either bank. The former railway track bed now leads straight back to Richmond, very much on the level. Just before reaching the old station buildings, there is a row of attractive railway cottages on the left. Bear right to return to the car park.

21

Swaledale: Reeth & Marrick Priory

Length: 5½ miles

Rise and Fall: Almost 250 feet in total. The 200 yards of uphill road on the return half, and the last rise to the centre of Reeth are the only ascents of any significance. The latter can be avoided by finding a parking place at the bottom of the village, nearer to the bridge.

Underfoot: Good overall. A very small amount of surfaced road, some good paths and considerable lengths of farm pasture-land.

Car Parking: Reeth village green (but see "rise and fall" above). Grid reference: 038992.

Map: Ordnance Survey Outdoor Leisure No. 30 Yorkshire Dales, Northern and Central areas. 1 : 25000

Description

Reeth is a large, stone-built, village strategically situated close to the junction of the Swale and Arkengarth Dales. At its heart is a large, often wind-swept, green. As the unofficial "capital" of middle to upper Swaledale, it has varied shops, catering, and other visitor facilities. It also has the small bur interesting Swaledale Folk Museum, where the history of local lead mining is given suitable prominence.

Marrick Priory was founded by Benedictine sisters in 1154, surviving until the Dissolution under King Henry VIII. It later became the parish church before its present use as an outdoor education and residential centre commenced in the 1960s.

Route

Follow the main road downhill to the bridge over Arkle Beck. Cross, and continue for about 50 yards to a kissing gate on the right, with a "Grinton" signpost. The well-used track is alongside the beck at first, soon bearing left to cross the broad river meadows, generous in extent by the standards of Swaledale. The route is easy to Grinton Bridge, where three arches span the River Swale.

Go up the steps, cross the road, and carry on along the river bank, reassured by a small sign. This path gives the impression of a more than usually gentle Swaledale, with river banks pleasantly lined with ash, sycamore and willow. A slight rise leads to a surfaced road. Bear right to continue to Marrick Priory. The tower of the former church is visible from afar. Less attractive is a scattering of old static caravans, which obviously slipped through the net of the Town and Country Planning Acts.

Unfortunately, there isn't really very much to admire at Marrick Priory unless you enjoy archaeological detective work. The remains of the Priory buildings have been "imaginatively converted into a residential centre in the late 1960s" according to a notice on the gate. Just a few pieces of original stonework stand clear of the conversion. The site is further complicated by the superimposition of a range of farm buildings and what can only be described as a large corrugated iron shack. An ancient mill dam lies above the Priory; nearby is a seat placed by the local Tourist Association in conjunction with the Turner Society. In this area there are other places where the great painter worked during his northern tour of 1816 and which have been similarly commemorated.

Reeth

The return route starts at a gate on the right of the roadway as you face back towards Reeth. There is no visible track for much of the next 1¼ miles, but proceed diagonally across the meadow keeping clear of the nearby fence. Aim for the stile with a yellow arrow in the wall ahead. The view is undoubtedly enhanced by the slight extra elevation of this return route. The way goes from stile to stile, usually with little gates attached, keeping a fairly straight line. At a wall corner with a farm gate, take the ladder stile in front, soon reaching a conventional stile 30 yards from a farm building. Do not go through the farm gate on the left but continue over three further stiles. As a road becomes obvious to the right, above, bend a little left to descend and rejoin the Marrick Priory lane at a stile.

Turn right, and then sharp right at the nearby road junction. Climb steeply for 200 yards, then turn left at a stile signposted "Fremington" Again, the path is not distinct on the ground, but follows a more or less straight line to Fremington with stiles at each cross wall. The village of Grinton with its imposing old church, shows up well on the left. The track keeps its line to pass well above Sorrel Sykes Farm to an old lane leading into Higher Fremington. At a surfaced lane turn left and then bear right, downhill.

As the road dips more steeply left, fork right at a farm gate, where the footpath sign is partially concealed by trees. Follow a broad, grassy, track with Reeth now in full view ahead. As the track bends right, uphill, stay alongside the wall, descending towards the main road, with more stiles, and the path obvious. Turn right to return to the village centre.

Folk museum, Reeth

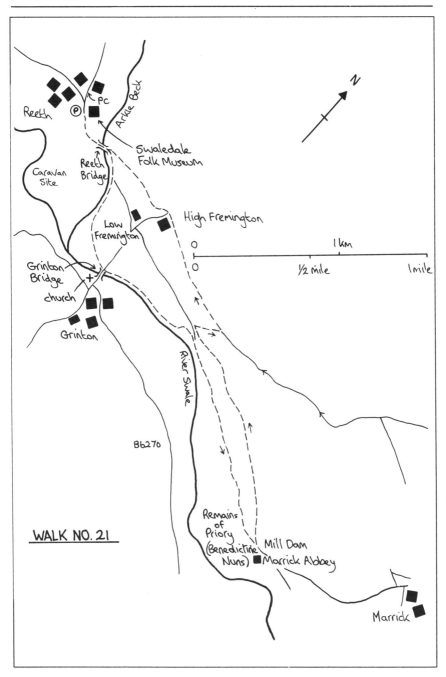

Reeth

PC

Arkle Beck

Swaledale
Folk Museum

Caravan
Site

Reeth
Bridge

Low
Fremington

High Fremington

0

0

1 km

½ mile

1 mile

Grinton
Bridge

church

Grinton

River Swale

B6270

WALK NO. 21

N

Remains
of
Priory
(Benedictine
Nuns)

Mill Dam

Marrick Abbey

Marrick

22

Arkengarthdale: Langthwaite circular

Length: 3¾ miles

Rise and Fall: Less than 150 feet in total. The most significant rise is along the road from Langthwaite to the church. No steep gradients.

Underfoot: Small section of wet/rough ground, otherwise good. Some surfaced private driveway and a small amount of road.

Car Parking: There is limited car parking space in the middle of Langthwaite, but plenty of roadside spaces by the Wesleyan chapel and the parish church, both on the main road.

Map: Ordnance Survey Outdoor Leisure No. 30 Yorkshire Dales, Northern and Central areas. 1:25000.

Description

Arkengarthdale is Swaledale's principal tributary valley, the Arkle Beck, rising on the bleak moors to the north, joining the River Swale close to Reeth. In conjunction with its better known neighbour it was a lead mining area of great importance for many centuries and it is not difficult to find the evidence of this widespread industry. Whilst much of the dale and its various tributaries have the stark, wide open, windswept appearance so typical of the lead mining uplands, the route of this walk passes through some surprisingly attractive wooded country, graced by properties of some stature, such as Scar House.

Langthwaite itself is a tight knit cluster around the inn and the shop. Televising of James Herriot's veterinary books has brought some fame to the village, the bridge being used for the opening sequence; a nearby water-splash on the road over to Low Moor has also been much featured.

The walk stays close to the valley bottom, keeping ups and downs to a minimum, but there is a fair variety within its comparatively short length.

Route

Leave the main road by the side of the trim, well-kept, parish church and follow the driveway towards Scar House. After West House, as the drive bends right to cross the beck, carry straight on to a stile over a stone wall. Turn left at the rough surfaced lane, soon bending right through a farm gate to a minor road. Eskeleth hamlet is uphill to the left. The octagonal building is a former gunpowder store, for obvious reasons standing alone in the middle of a field.

Former gunpowder store

Cross the road diagonally to the gap in the wall opposite, signposted "Whaw 1¼ miles". The path is along the side of the Arkle Beck, turning sharp left by the end of a wooden footbridge, up a moderately steep bank, to a little gate by the end of a row of restored cottages. Pass along the front of the cottages to a farm gate and a good, broad, track falling gently towards Swallow Holm. The right of way passes to the left of the house, then bears a little to the right towards a wall, where a rudimentary track is evident. Follow this down to the bank of the beck to reach a wooden bridge, with gate, over a tributary stream, rising a little on the far side. The path, now lumpy underfoot and with a wet section, contours above the beck before descending again to a footbridge. Wood House stands out on the far bank, a gaunt stone building, entirely in harmony with the overall landscape of this part of the Dales.

Cross the footbridge, turn right at a narrow but distinct footpath, and rise towards a stile to enter an area of dense woodland with boulders and thick undergrowth. Leave the woodland by a small gate. Yealand House is on the

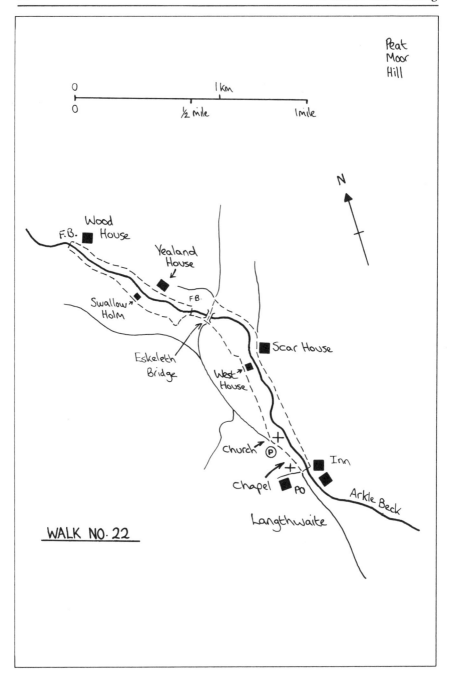

Peat
Moor
Hill

N

Wood
F.B. House
Yealand
House
Swallow
Holm
F.B.
Eskeleth
Bridge
Scar House
West
House
Church
Chapel
PO
Inn
Arkle Beck
Langthwaite

WALK NO. 22

left as the path continues by a gate and stiles to another footbridge over the Arkle Beck. High on the left is the well-scarred bulk of Peat Moor Hill, almost 1700 feet in height. Cross the bridge and turn left to rejoin the minor road near Stang Bridge. Turn left to cross the bridge.

At the road junction in 100 yards, turn right over a stile with a signpost "Langthwaite 1 mile". A grassy path heads for Scar House, passing a faint yellow mark on a rock, crossing a small stream to a stile, and climbing to a gate which gives access to the landscaped gardens. At the Scar House drive turn right for only a short distance, then left to pass along the front of a building, to a farm gate with yellow marker and stile. The path ahead is just visible on the grass as it heads straight back to Langthwaite, a little up and down but entirely without complication. Cross the bridge in Langthwaite and turn right to return to the car parking places by the chapel or the parish church.

Langthwaite church

Gunnerside

23

Swaledale: Gunnerside Circular

Length: 2¾ miles

Rise and Fall: about 100 feet, half of which occurs in one stretch on the main valley road after crossing the river.

Underfoot: One mile on surfaced road, otherwise good field paths.

Car Parking: There is parking for several vehicles close to the road bridge in Gunnerside. Grid reference: 951982

Map: Ordnance Survey Outdoor Leisure No. 30 Yorkshire Dales, Northern and Central areas. 1:25000

Description

This gentle little walk is based on Gunnerside, a village with a long and important history of lead mining, the tributary valley of Gunnerside Gill being scattered with the remains of this industry. Many of the solid stone houses of the village are former miners' cottages. The facilities include an inn, restaurant/cafe, post office stores, and public conveniences. There are no refreshments along the way, but the bank of the river below Ivelet has delectable spots for picnics.

Route

From the road junction by the bridge in Gunnerside, start along the road towards Muker, with Gunnerside Gill on the left, soon crossing the River Swale and bending right, rising 50 feet or so. Continue along the road to the hamlet of Satron.

Where the road narrows, turn right into an unsignposted path, just before Satron Cottage. There is a lane on the opposite side of the main road. A grassy track between walls leads to a stile on the left. Take this and follow a partially paved track across a meadow. At the far side take the right-hand of two stiles and bear right along a well-trodden path. After passing farm buildings make for a stile and gate and descend steeply towards the river, carrying on to a stile which gives access to a surfaced lane.

Turn right to cross Ivelet Bridge, a beautifully arched packhorse bridge of 1695, and follow the lane along the side of the river to Ivelet hamlet. At the public telephone box turn right at a "public footpath to Gunnerside" sign, and bear right at a yellow arrow to cross Shore Gill, dipping and rising quite steeply for a few feet. The track is well-used and always clear on the ground, crossing stone walls at frequent intervals by the tightly-pinching stiles so typical of this part of the Yorkshire Dales. A combination of short legs and plump posterior can pose some difficulty unless help is at hand!

The path is raised sufficiently above the valley bottom to provide good views down and across the valley, but is basically a level route. A slight descent towards the river is followed by bearing left towards Gunnerside, entered through a small modern housing complex.

Ivelet Bridge, Swaledale

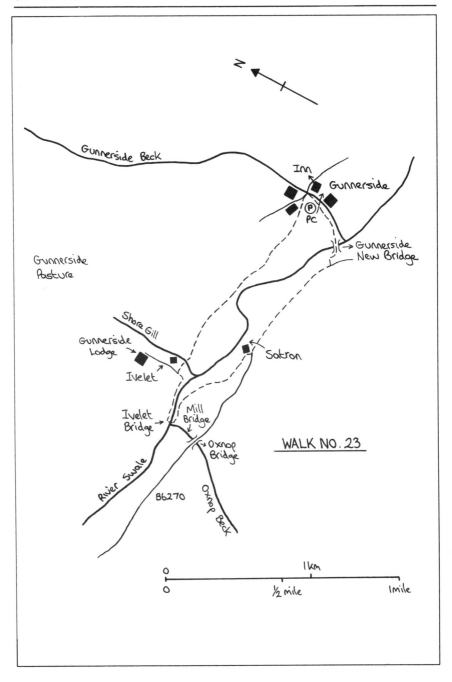

WALK NO. 23

A fine pair of tups near Keld

24

Swaledale: Keld & Muker

Length: 4½ miles (Keld to Oxnop Bridge)

Rise and Fall: As Keld is a good deal higher than Muker or Oxnop Bridge, this is, overall, a downhill walk. However, from Keld there is an initial climb of 70 or 80 feet and a few other small rises along the way.

Underfoot: Some rough and stony footpath, otherwise good, grassy, tracks.

Car Parking: Public car parking at Muker, grid reference: 911978, and at Keld, grid reference: 893013.

Map: Ordnance Survey Outdoor Leisure No. 30, Yorkshire Dales, Northern and Central areas. 1:25000.

Description

Keld is a small village, its stone buildings close huddled in countering the severity of the climate at an altitude of more than 1000 feet. Close by is possibly the finest part of upper Swaledale, with the river tumbling over falls, beside steep rocky walls and overhanging trees. The Pennine Way and the Coast to Coast long distance footpaths intersect near to Keld, a walkers' crossroads of great significance.

The bulk of Keld Hill separates Keld from Muker, which is at a lower level and has more facilities for visitors including a post office/stores and an inn. However, Muker is still comparatively high in Swaledale, a farming village of very compact form. Until the present church was built in 1580, local deaths necessitated an arduous journey to Grinton along the "corpse road", a situation common to many Dales hamlets and small villages for several centuries. The opening of Swaledale Woollens has brought about a modern revival of the traditional hand knitting cottage industry of the dale.

The beautifully arched Ivelet packhorse bridge spans the Swale just below the hamlet of the same name. A little further is the now defunct Mill Bridge which carried the valley road over Oxnop Beck before the present Oxnop Bridge was constructed in comparatively modern times.

In such spectacularly hilly country a circuit for "level" walkers is not possible. The suggested linear route can be terminated at Muker (2½ miles) or Oxnop Bridge (4½ miles) or, indeed, at Gunnerside (5½ miles). There appear to be three possible methods of achieving the walk, which is highly recommended to all lovers of fine Dales scenery:

1) To use two vehicles, one at each end.

2) To use the local bus (Tuesdays and Saturdays only – check the times)

3) To have a non-walking driver in the party.

Note: the direct route from Muker to Ivelet Bridge does involve a potentially awkward crossing of the River Swale. If the river is high, this will not be possible to achieve dry-footed, and the longer way, back-tracking to Ramps Holme Bridge or, of course, using that bridge to by-pass Muker altogether, will then be necessary.

Muker

Route

Set off along the well-used track leaving Keld at the bottom right corner of the square, downhill at first but soon rising steadily to its junction with the Pennine Way.

[Note: There is a little path on the left which leads to Kisdon Force. This is a diversion through fine rock and river scenery but there is a steep descent on a narrow path and you do have to come back the same way].

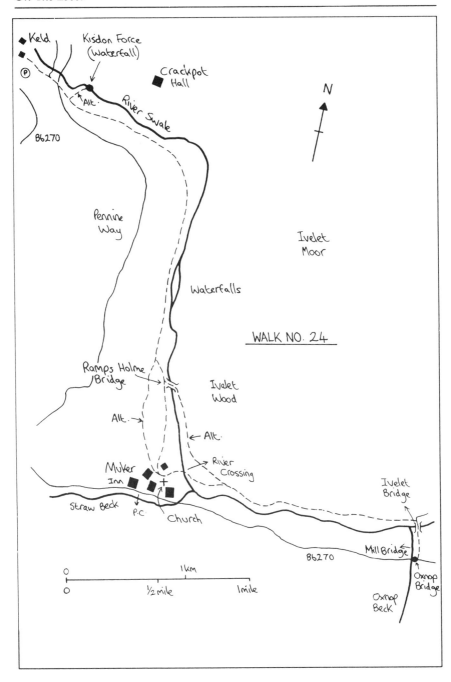

Keld

Kisdon Force
(Waterfall)

Crackpot
Hall

P

Alt

River Swale

B6270

N

Pennine
Way

Ivelet
Moor

Waterfalls

WALK NO. 24

Ramps Holme
Bridge

Ivelet
Wood

Alt.

Alt.

River
Crossing

Muker
Inn

Ivelet
Bridge

Straw Beck

P.C.

Church

B6270

Mill Bridge

Ivelet
Bridge

Oxnop
Bridge

0   1km

0   ½ mile   1 mile

Oxnop
Beck

The track soon forks left, signposted to Muker, descending gently towards that village through grassy meadows and passing dilapidated farm buildings. There are stiles and yellow marks to aid navigation, but the way is clear on the ground all the way along this superb footpath.

Muker comes into view, followed by Ramps Holme Bridge over the River Swale and then a fork and choice of route. For the direct route to Ivelet Bridge or the flat route to Muker, bear left towards the visible bridge. For a more uphill route to Muker, bear right. The flat route to Muker is alongside a stone wall, reaching a stile on the right with a "Muker" signpost, short of the bridge. The way into the village is now evident.

From Muker the "direct" route is a little tricky. As you enter the village, bear left to pass through a yard between buildings to a farm gate. There is no signpost. The path is faintly visible on the ground as it stays close to a wall on the left-hand side, descends a little bank to a stile on the left, then diagonally to a stile ahead, bending right towards the river. Another stile gives access to the river bank, with some dense undergrowth. There are no official stepping stones across the river, but those with good balance should find little difficulty in dry weather. A little way downstream is probably the best line to take.

On reaching the far side, with wet or dry feet, a track is joined behind the angle of a ruined wall. Turn right. Cross to the far side of the wall at an opening and aim for a stile with a yellow mark ahead. This path is not well-used, but joins the better-used track from Ramps Holme Bridge by the stile.

As a choice of stiles is apparent, take that on the right to stay closer to the river along a delightful grassy path, with oak, beech, and willow in profusion. A steep sided length of river necessitates a short, steep, climb up the river bank to a stile and then a gate. The meadows beyond are overrun with rabbit warrens. The path slants away from the river towards a gate before Ivelet Bridge, with its welcoming seat is approached. (For a description of the bridge and the further continuation of the walk to Gunnerside, see Walk 23, Gunnerside). Turn right over the bridge past possible picnic areas followed by the ruin of Mill Bridge immediately before the main road is reached. The hamlet of Satron is half a mile to the left.

<u>25</u>

Middleham and Coverham

Length: 4½ miles

Rise and Fall: 550 feet in total, divided into three main sections. Apart from the short rise after Hullo Bridge, all gradients are easy.

Underfoot: Three quarters of a mile of very minor road, otherwise good paths and routes across farmland.

Car Parking: Market Square, Middleham. Grid reference: 128877

Map: Ordnance Survey Outdoor Leisure No. 30, Northern and Central areas. 1 : 25000

Description

Middleham is an ancient little town of rare distinction, with its great old castle as the dominant feature. Richard Plantagenet, marrying into the Neville family and later becoming Duke of Gloucester, lived here as a boy and young man until, in 1483, he succeeded to the throne as King Richard III. Killed at Bosworth Field in 1485, he has long been regarded as a hunchbacked out-and-out villain, as portrayed by Shakespeare. More recent opinion is inclined to a more balanced view of Richard. During his years at Middleham as "Lord of the North", he kept law and order over the region and defended against the Scots. His devotion turned Middleham into a place of learning through the foundation of a collegiate church.

Formerly referred to as the "Windsor of the North", the castle also has the distinction that two Kings, Edward IV and Henry VI, were imprisoned here at different times; truly, as put by English Heritage who now look after the castle, "one of the great seats of power in the 15th century".

From the early 19th century, of the greatest importance to the town has been the presence of several horse racing stables in the vicinity, with the Low and High Middleham Moors providing wide open spaces for gallops.

Coverdale Abbey was founded in the 13th century by the Premonstratensian Order, was pillaged by the Scots in 1331 but recovered to carry on until dissolution in 1548. Braithwaite Hall of the 17th century is now a working farm with 748 acres of moor and farmland, owned by the National Trust. Public visiting is allowed, by arrangement with the tenant.

The walk is a varied circuit, rather up and down but nowhere difficult, packed with interesting features throughout its short length.

Route

From the square at Middleham head towards the castle and follow the broad lane (Canaan Lane) past this magnificent structure. Fifty yards past the castle turn right at a small gap in the wall to go diagonally across rough ground to a stile at the far side, followed by a second stile under a large tree. Stay with the path along the side of the Coverham road. Up to the left is the site of Middleham's first castle, a ring and bailey on a prominent mound known as William's Hill, originally occupied by a Danish invader named Ghulpstrick or Ghilpatrick. For closer examination, this mound can be visited by using a track which branches off Canaan Lane a little further to the south.

Middleham Castle

Continue until a gap in the wall on the right necessitates joining Coverham Lane. It is no hardship to walk along the ample grassy verge until a signpost is reached by a corner in the wall. This signpost offers both a bridleway and a footpath. Pinker's Pond, attractively backed by exposed limestone and trees, is close on the right, while beyond are the gallop areas of Middleham Low and High Moors.

Take the footpath, which stays close to the road for about 300 yards. Go through a field gate and aim diagonally right. There is a stile with yellow

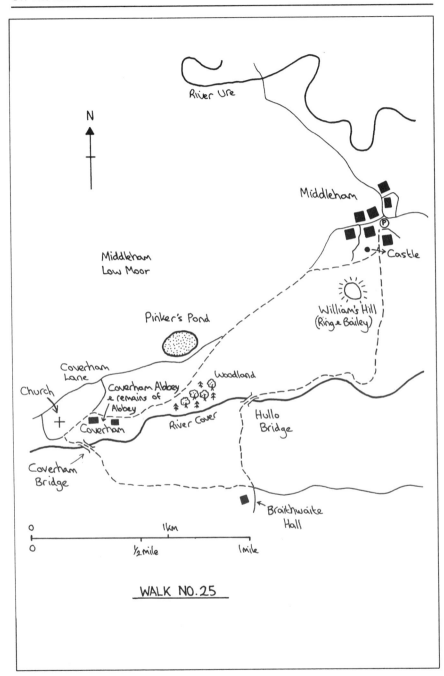

WALK NO.25

arrow close to the right-hand end of the plantation below. Pass through the woodland, cross a small stream, and climb over a broken gate into a meadow at a point where there should be a stile. In 40 yards descend to the left along a track in a shallow depression, towards the River Cover. This track has a very ancient appearance, with the remains of stone walls on either side; it could well have been associated with the nearby former Abbey. A gate into a meadow is beside a ruined building, with a stone-covered culvert beyond. Perhaps this was the Abbey Mill?

The route veers towards the right-hand boundary of the meadow, soon reaching a farm lane to the right of the buildings, with the tower of Coverdale church in view ahead. Some surviving portions of the Priory structure are entangled with more modern farm and residential buildings, but the area is still full of interest. A short diversion to the right is necessary if you wish to visit the church.

Cross Coverdale Bridge and follow the quiet lane signposted "East Witton and Masham". Beside Coverdale Bridge is a fine and accessible picnic spot by the river. The lane climbs considerably but at a reasonable gradient to reach a large farm close to Braithwaite Hall. The views over Coverdale certainly make the effort worthwhile.

Coverdale Abbey

Directly opposite the Braithwaite Hall drive turn left to take the "bridle-way to Hullo Bridge ⅓ml" and follow this well-defined track downhill to the solid little bridge, which spans a very attractive length of the river with much exposed rock. Turn right over a stile 20 yards after the bridge, and slant up the river bank: steepish but short, and good underfoot. Continue along the bottom edge of a field, bend left to aim for the upper end of some conifers, gently rising, and choose either stile to carry on along the side of the fence.

As the rudimentary path begins to drop towards the river, bend left to avoid any significant descent, and then turn left as a path rising from the riverside is met. It is, however, worth a short diversion to look at the cliffs on the far side of the river. The broad grassy track now points directly back to Middleham, rising gently by the side of the broken wall/fence field boundary. A stile leads to the last little rise with the wall now on the left as the castle in all its glory suddenly bursts into view. The long view includes Leyburn town as the path descends to Canaan Lane and Middleham.

26

Leyburn Shawl and Wensley

Length: 6¼ miles

Rise and Fall: Approximately 500 feet in total, divided between the climb out of Leyburn to the top of the shawl and the more gradual return from Wensley to Leyburn. No steep gradients.

Underfoot: No difficulties, but some routes across farmland are not distinct on the ground. There is a very small amount of road walking.

Car Parking: Market Square or pay and display car park in Leyburn. Grid reference: 112905

Map: Ordnance Survey Outdoor Leisure No. 30 Yorkshire Dales, Northern and Central areas. 1:25000

Description

Leyburn is a bustling little town, probably seen at its best on Fridays, when the spacious square is filled with market stalls. Shops, banks, cafes and inns are plentiful. It is now the undisputed "capital" of lower Wensleydale, but it was not always so. Wensley had a market charter from 1207 and was much the most important centre in the area until the Black Death struck in 1563. Subsequently, Wensley lost out both to Askrigg and to Leyburn, which gained its charter in 1684.

Present day Wensley is nothing more than a quiet village, but unfortunate in having the main road passing through. It has assumed the character of an "estate" village since the construction of Bolton Hall in 1678. Despite renovations, the church of 1300 or so, built in local stone, is still handsome and has much of interest inside. A former water mill is now home to White Rose Candles, open to the public for retail sales, whilst the Three Horse Shoes Inn provides refreshment.

The present walk is an excellent circuit linking the town and the village, using the famous Shawl as an outward route. It is claimed that Mary, Queen of Scots was recaptured on The Shawl following her escape from captivity in Bolton Castle, nearby. The actual spot is known as Queen's Gap, said to be identified by walls at either side of the track. A sign has gone and only a small pile of stones remains.

The former Wensleydale railway, described more fully in Walk 28 , was kept open as far as Redmire until early 1994 for the transport of the stone from the nearby quarry. Alas, this traffic has ceased; presumably a replacement fleet of lorries now uses the narrow roads along the valley.

Route

From the upper portion of Leyburn market place take the cul de sac road signposted to "The Shawl", pass the old fire station and quickly leave the built-up area by an old kissing gate. A footpath trodden by generations of local strollers ascends above the long limestone scarp with the curious name. As height is gained there are long views over the wide expanse of lower Wensleydale and to the long flat top of Penhill. The route is entirely straightforward, much of it fringed by trees, with ash predominant.

To the right, Moor Quarry is unsightly but is, mostly, well-screened; there has been some additional tree planting in recent years. After almost a mile from Leyburn the track passes between stone walls about 10 feet apart.

On Leyburn Shawl

Below was an old railway access to the quarry, with an inclined plane plunging down to connect with the Wensleydale railway. There were sid-

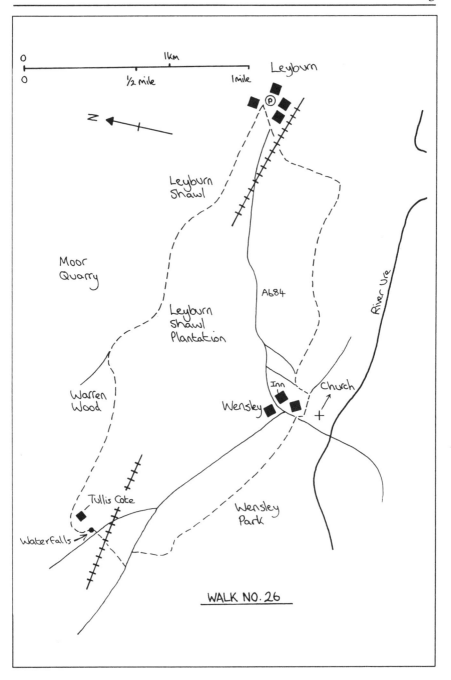

Leyburn

0 ────────── 1km
0 ────────── 1mile
½ mile

N

Leyburn
Shawl

Moor
Quarry

Leyburn
Shawl
Plantation

A684

River Ure

Warren
Wood

Inn

Church

Wensley

Tullis Cote

Wensley
Park

Waterfalls

WALK NO. 26

ings and overhead loading facilities at the bottom, some remains of which can still be seen by the adventurous.

Continue past Leyburn Shawl plantation until the track divides beside a gateway which leads into the quarry. Fork left, downhill, along the bottom edge of Warren Wood for less than 200 yards, then angle across the large field towards a gate in the bottom corner. The wildlife in this area includes rabbits and pheasants. From the gate a broad farm track continues along the edge of several fields to Tullis Cote Farm,

Pass the farm, with its large modern outbuildings, and turn left at a junction of trackways, downhill, beside a wooded valley with waterfalls on the right. Turn right at the next junction to follow the rough-surfaced farm road, winding downhill. On the left is a substantial ruin, obviously some kind of mill, with its chimney high on the bank above. Fork right to reach the public road.

Go straight across to a footpath which crosses the railway line, the former Wensley station being visible to the left, before reaching another public road. Turn left for 200 yards and then right at a "public footpath" sign. Follow the broad driveway for less than 50 yards and then turn left at a signposted footpath. A gate with a yellow arrow points the way generally along the boundary of a large field. Avoid a projecting spur of woodland and keep the

The River Ure at Wensley

same line, downhill, past ruined buildings, and across the wide open space of the Wensley Park land which surrounds Bolton Hall. There is little to see on the ground, but aim for a gate in the bottom right corner close to the point where woodland meets the estate roadway. Go through the gate and turn left to reach Wensley village.

Head for the church, turning left and then left again along a lane which turns sharp right and then left. Just after the left bend, turn right through a gate and go straight across a field and through a stile. Keep close to the field boundary, but after the next stile angle left towards the edge of the woodland ahead. Continue via several arrowed stiles, passing Leyburn Old Glebe Nature Reserve. Leyburn comes into view as more fields are crossed. Aim to the left of a farm building, then turn sharp left along the hedgerow above the building. Follow this hedgerow towards a wooden gate at the railway line, but cross the line by three ladder stiles, then angling right, uphill, to walk by the side of the main road back to Leyburn.

27

Aysgarth and West Burton

Length: 4½ miles.

Rise and Fall: 340 feet. The majority of the ascent occurs on the final part of the walk, by the side of the River Ure; there are two short but steep sections.

Underfoot: Short lengths of surfaced road; otherwise good field paths.

Car Parking: Privately owned car park (charge payable) close to the youth hostel on the road leading down to the Aysgarth Falls. Grid reference 012884.

Map: Ordnance Survey Outdoor Leisure No. 30 Yorkshire Dales, Northern and Central areas. 1 : 25000

Description

This is a walk packed with good things. Without appearing "manicured" or to have a contrived prettiness, West Burton is rightly acclaimed as a good example of a village, with old stone cottages flanking a generous green, and an inn and shops to serve local needs. The present cross on the green, erected in 1820 and restored in 1889, marks the site of a much older market; the waterfall and its immediate vicinity are delightful.

The final part of the route has some of the best riverside scenery in the Dales, as it climbs along the top of the steep bank of the River Ure, accompanied by the constant roar of the water cascading over the steps of hard rock which give the Aysgarth Falls their essential character.

Close to the start of the walk is the much visited riverside by the higher Aysgarth Fall, where the substantial mill building has been converted into a carriage museum, with a craft centre, tea room, and gift shop adjacent. You can also sample the local Wensleydale cheese. Close by is a riverside picnic area, car park, cafe, and public conveniences. The descent to this tourist honeypot is steep and considerable and most "level" walkers will probably prefer to drive down to the National Park car park.

Route

From the car park turn left uphill to the main road. Turn left, again, downhill, along the road for about 150 yards to a stile on the right, to take a signposted footpath to "Eshington Bridge ½ mile". Descend gently across the meadow heading for a stile in the far wall, West Burton village soon coming into view ahead. Cross a sharp little dip and rise and then continue to descend steadily, helped by occasional yellow arrows, keeping the same line across a field where the path is not immediately apparent, to reach a little gate in the bottom corner, to the right of a farm building. Turn left at a stile, pass an electricity pole with a yellow arrow, to reach Eshington Lane at the bottom of the field.

Turn right across Eshington Bridge and, in 40 yards, turn right again at a stile signposted "West Burton ¾ mile". This footpath follows a straight line across good valley bottom farm land. After a third of a mile the path swings left at a stile with a yellow mark to head straight for the village. A minor road is reached at a gate and stile. Go across to ascend a few steps and follow a track into the village. The steps can be avoided by turning left along the minor road and then sharp right back into the village, but the detour is quite considerable. Back on course, turn right, uphill, to reach the spacious green, with post office store, inn, market cross and stocks.

So far, the whole of the route has followed the line of an old church footpath; for centuries, Aysgarth was the church serving the whole of a huge parish which included West Burton.

West Burton

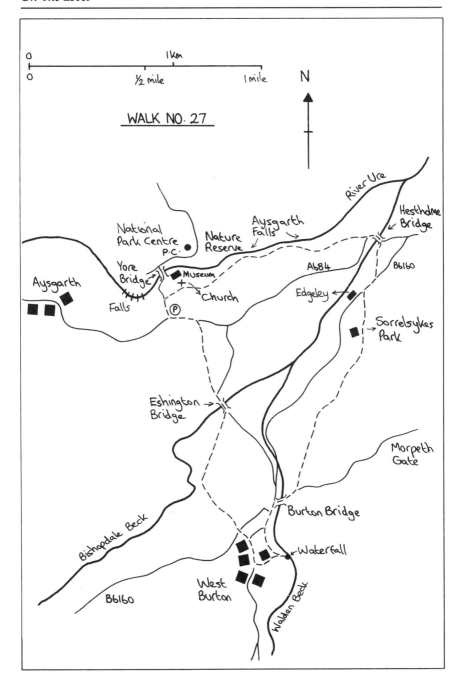

WALK NO. 27

Bear left across the bottom of the green and descend towards the Mill House. An essential detour of a few yards to the right brings the reward of a lovely glen-like area with waterfall, steep valley sides, exposed rock, former mill, and old packhorse bridge – a perfect picnic spot.

Waterfall, West Burton, Wensleydale

Return to the road and carry on downhill; between road and stream (Walden Beck) the gardens of houses terrace attractively down to the water. On the far side, a rising field appears to have evidence of a much older cultivation system. Join a more important road, continuing towards Aysgarth and Leyburn, then turn right immediately, over a packhorse bridge, to follow a lane for 200 yards or so. This lane is part of "Morpeth Gate", a medieval highway connecting Middleham Castle with the hunting forest of Bishop- dale, later used as a packhorse and, probably, a drovers' road. Turn left at a stile to take a footpath to "Edgeley". Although not well-marked on the ground, helped by occasional yellow marks and arrows the way is never in doubt as it crosses some of the broad acres of the flat Wensleydale valley bottom. The landscape is dominated by farming, with abundant field barns, visually improved by scattered trees and by a long scarp above on the right.

At a field barn bear a little to the right towards a farm gate, rise slightly past another barn to a second gate, to go left along the upper edge of a strip of woodland. Cross a stream, pass a finger post in a meadow, follow the indicated line, turn left downhill along a farm track, and then right along the edge of a field immediately at the bottom of the slope. The object here is to avoid the large farming complex of Sorrel Sykes Park: several posts, with or without yellow marks, give the line of the right of way. In view above on the right are the remains of an obelisk and other structures. Bear left to cross a field diagonally, towards Edgeley, which is situated on the far side of the road, aiming for a small gate in the stone wall.

Turn right to follow the road for a little over 100 yards. Turn left at a farm gate with a signpost "Hestholme Bridge 300m." The faint path heads for a patch of woodland, where a stile gives access to a path leading to Hestholme Bridge. Cross the bridge and then turn right, over the stile, and head for the River Ure, welcomed by the increasing roar of the Aysgarth lower falls. The return path is now unmistakeable, generally rising along the top of the steep river bank, the magnificent river scenery helping to make light of the most strenuous part of the walk. Two sections are quite steep, but in each case the rise is limited to less than 40 feet. As the path leaves the riverside, it traverses a dense plantation, emerging close to Aysgarth parish church. Cross the churchyard and turn left at the road to return to the car park.

Askrigg

28

Askrigg Circular

Length: 2½ miles.

Rise and Fall: 100 feet approximately not including the detour to the waterfall. No steep ascent.

Underfoot: half a mile on surfaced road; remainder on generally good field paths.

Car Parking: In Askrigg village, off-street in front of the church. Grid reference: 948910.

Map: Ordnance Survey Outdoor Leisure No. 30 Yorkshire Dales, Northern and Central areas. 1:25000.

Description

Askrigg is an ancient settlement, once the most important town of Upper Wensleydale, but losing out to Hawes when the latter gained its own market charter, in 1699, and a later turnpike road. The market cross, by the church, is a reminder of these greater days. Fame of a different sort has come in more recent times with the filming of various parts of James Herriot's veterinary stories involving several buildings in this still attractive village.

Mill Gill Force is one of the best of the lesser-known Yorkshire Dales waterfalls, the rushing water of this stream having powered no less than three mills (still visible) close to Askrigg. The present walk passes by two of these mills.

The Askrigg portion of the former Wensleydale railway was closed to passengers in 1954 and to goods traffic in 1964, the track being lifted in 1965. There is still considerable regret at this loss and the Wensleydale Railway Association has been formed, with the intention of opening at least some of the line for tourist purposes. It has to be said that in the area around the former Askrigg station the prospects appear to be far from promising.

Route

Follow a roadway signposted to "Mill Gill Force", along the upper side of the parish church, the road soon losing its surface. At the entrance gate to Mill Gill House fork right at a little gate and cross the field to reach an old mill with an overhead metal leat still in situ. Cross the gill by the footbridge and rise to the right into woodland at a "Mill Gill Force" signpost. The path is rather steep here, but soon becomes more level as it keeps to the top of the steep, wooded valley side, squeezed against a stone wall.

Mill Gill Force comes into view. At a signposted junction of paths, a short diversion to view the fall at close range is recommended. To continue from the junction, the left fork leads to a stile from which a trackway used by farm vehicles keeps a few yards to the right of a stone wall. The elevation gives good long views across Wensleydale. On reaching a lane, turn left to descend to the Askrigg road, turning left again to pass a row of buildings on the right. Forty yards after the last building turn sharp right at a stile signposted "Bainbridge ¾ mile" and follow a paved path towards the railway embankment. Turn left at a farm track just before an attractive footbridge and, immediately after the railway embankment, turn left at a little gate into a narrow footpath. A straight line is now followed for some distance beside or on the old railway line.

The former Askrigg goods yard now houses an untidy industrial site with scattered rubbish and unsightly temporary buildings comparing very unfavourably with the dignified stonework of the former goods shed and platform buildings, still in good condition after years of neglect.

After the station, turn left to rejoin the road, turning right towards Askrigg. Look out for a footpath on the left at a stile with rudimentary stone steps. This paved path rises across a field towards the church, passing a compact area of most attractive old cottages on the way back to the parking area.

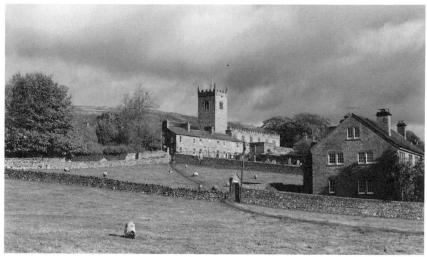

Askrigg church

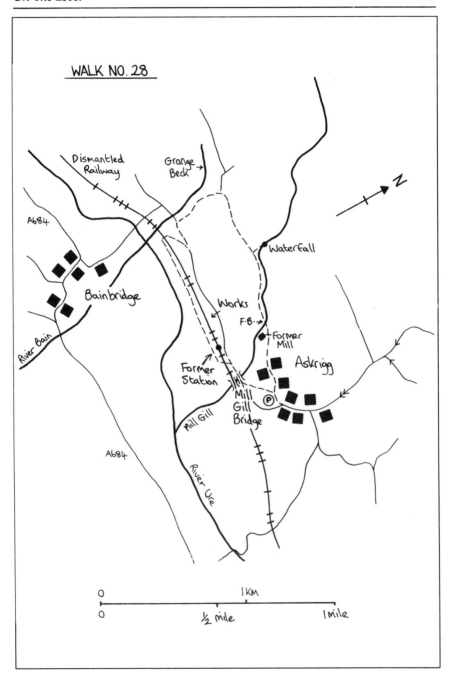

29

Semerwater and Marsett

Length: 4 miles

Rise and Fall: about 200 feet, mostly on the return route (surfaced lane) with one rather steep section.

Underfoot: A little more than 1½ miles on surfaced but very quiet lane. Otherwise a mixture of field paths, some likely to be muddy in wet weather.

Car Parking: On the "beach" at the foot of Semerwater. Grid reference: 922876

Map: Ordnance Survey Outdoor Leisure No. 30 Yorkshire Dales, Northern and Central areas. 1:25000.

Description

Although comparatively little-known, Raydale is a fair sized tributary valley of Wensleydale, with the most unusual feature of Semerwater. Indeed, with a circumference of three miles, Semerwater is the largest lake in the northern part of the Yorkshire Dales. Following the end of the last period of glaciation some 10,000 years ago, the lake was much larger, having been formed behind a dam of naturally-deposited glacial material. It is now used for water sports such as wind surfing and canoe training for school parties. The small beach at the north-eastern end provides an excellent car parking/family picnic area. The outgoing River Bain, which joins the River Ure at Bainbridge, is claimed to be the shortest river in England.

Apart from its lake, Raydale has scenery fairly typical of the northern dales, with stone walls and barns, although much of the valley bottom above the lake is obviously badly drained giving poor quality farming land. Road access to the dale is limited to two very minor cul de sacs, one to the farming hamlet of Stalling Busk and the other reaching 1½ miles further up the valley to Raydale House after serving Marsett.

Within its modest distance, the present walk provides a good sample of Raydale; there are no refreshments available en route.

Route

From the car park turn right along the lane, up and over a rise for a distance of about 300 yards, then turn right over a ladder stile signposted "Stalling

Busk 1 mile" to follow a not very well-defined path across a field, aiming for a stile in the wall at the far side. After two further stiles a farm building is reached and the path descends to the edge of the lake. After the lake, a gently rising path continues along Raydale, windswept and bleak, with just a few stunted hawthorns and field barns, both used and derelict. The remains of a long abandoned church sit sadly within its graveyard, the enclosing walls still sound, unlike those of the church itself which are obviously potentially dangerous.

Abandoned church near Stalling Busk

In a further 40 yards, the path forks: the route to the left rises to Stalling Busk, visible on the skyline. This would make a reasonable extension of the walk for those who are happy with the obvious ascent. Our main route bears right, signposted to "Marsett" and crossing a small stream to a stile, soon reaching another stile in a wall above a farm building, then crossing more fields, always heading for a stile on the far side.

At a stile between a farm building and the huge stump of an old tree, turn sharp right to follow a vague path close to the left side of a wall, heading across the valley towards the now visible village of Marsett. This turning can easily be missed. If so, a stony lane (Busk Lane) is reached. A right turn here heads for Marsett, but the beck ahead must be crossed at a shallow ford; at most times of the year, wet feet would be the likely penalty of this mis-navigation! The correct path reaches a stile in the wall on the right (yellow marker), bears left to a modern footbridge, joins Busk Lane, and crosses another footbridge to continue to Marsett. Along this section the impressive head of Raydale is well seen.

Marsett is a no nonsense farming hamlet, its appearance making no concessions to prettiness or to the likely opinions of visitors.

From Marsett bear right to cross the bridge and follow the road (Marsett Lane) back along the valley towards Countersett and Bainbridge. This is a very quiet lane, making a perfectly satisfactory return route, with good views across the valley to the steep-ended hill top of Addlebrough (1564 feet) and some steep edges above on the left. The road does rise and fall somewhat, but the gradients are never really steep. Before reaching the foot of the steepest downhill, turn right at a stile with a "Semerwater Bridge" signpost. The path is rather indistinct but heads directly for the lake edge car park, through a gate with a yellow mark, then stunted lake edge woodland, to emerge by the shapely Semerwater Bridge. Turn right to reach the car park.

Semerwater

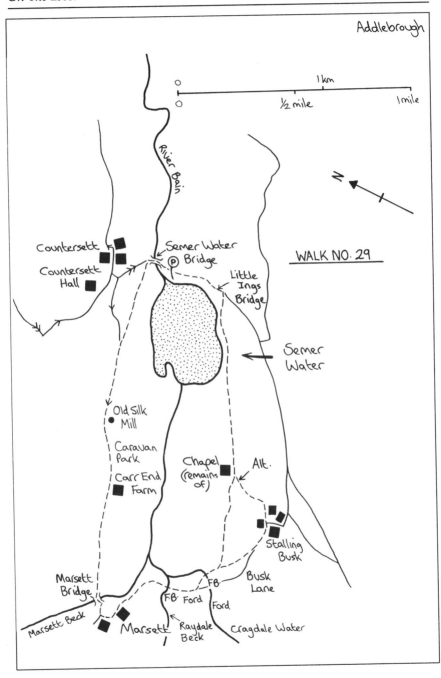

Addlebrough

1 km
½ mile   1 mile

River Bain

N

Countersett

Countersett Hall

Semer Water Bridge

P

Little Ings Bridge

WALK NO. 29

Semer Water

Old Silk Mill

Caravan Park

Carr End Farm

Chapel (remains of)

Alt.

Stalling Busk

Marsett Bridge

Busk Lane

F.B.

F.B. Ford

Ford

Marsett Beck

Marsett

Raydale Beck

Cragdale Water

30

Hawes, Gayle & Burtersett

Length: 3 miles

Rise and Fall: 130 feet, in one continuous but not steep ascent, right at the outset.

Underfoot: About half a mile on surfaced road. Remainder on predominantly good field paths and lane. The lane is likely to be muddy in wet weather.

Car Parking: Close to the bridge at Gayle. Grid reference: 872893

Map: Ordnance Survey Outdoor Leisure No. 30 Yorkshire Dales, Northern and Central areas. 1:25000

Description

Gayle is a substantial village, situated barely half a mile from Hawes, with a mixture of good old houses and more mediocre modern development. The Gayle Beck, rushing noisily through the village, formerly powered a large mill, the building, complete with feeder leat, still being very obvious.

Gayle Mill

Although only a little further distant from Hawes, Burtersett has a much more remote feel; among the meadows its cottages climb a steep hillside, with the characteristic shape of Yorburgh high above. Originally a sheep farming settlement, the name indicating its Norse origin, it still has the appearance of a real unspoilt Dales village but, unfortunately, has no facilities for the purchase of refreshments. One claim to fame is that the family home of Sir Edmund Hillary, the first person to climb Mount Everest, is situated here.

Burtersett

Route

There is a signpost at one end of the parking area to "footpath Burtersett 1¼ml, Marsett 3ml". Go through the stile and follow a clear path rising across several meadows, separated by stone walls with stiles. After three fields the track bends left, the stile here having a signpost showing the parting of the ways, Burtersett being to the left along a now level route.

The views down and across the valley are good, although the large caravan site at Hawes and the smaller one nearby are blots on the landscape. Above, to the right, is the shapely hill top of Yorburgh, an outlying part of

Wether Fell, with intake walls high on the hillside showing the efforts made by previous generations of farmers to wring just a little more from this ungenerous land. A fast-flowing stream may pose problems in wet weather; if so, a diversion to the right will be necessary. The track continues to be clear and well-signposted, reaching a number of stone barns, following the last of which a lane (Shaws Lane) leads directly to the top end of Burtersett village.

The road through the village is steeply downhill. Below the village, turn left at a stile with a signpost "footpath Hawes and Gayle" to follow a paved track across a meadow. This excellent path goes from field to field in an almost straight line, with built-up stiles of a more than usually generous construction to cross each wall. It could be an old route whereby worshippers from Burtersett walked to and from the church at Hawes.

After approximately a third of a mile and immediately beyond a stile, the path forks, the paved route to the right going to Hawes. Our unpaved path goes straight on, crossing the caravan and camping fields, to stiles in the far walls, bending slightly right in each case. On reaching a minor road, turn left to return directly to the parking area. On the left of this road, look out for the mound of an ancient earthwork.

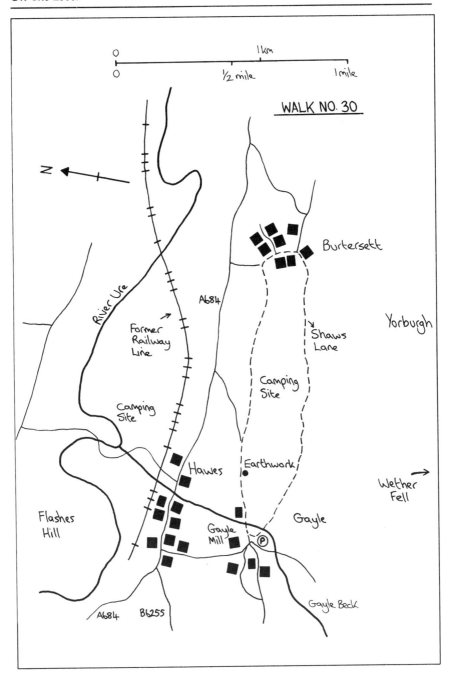

WALK NO. 30

31

Hawes & Appersett

Length: 5¼ miles

Rise and Fall: 300 feet approximately, well-spaced and with no really steep or prolonged ascent.

Underfoot: A wide variety, including two miles of surfaced road and lane, mostly very little used; also a length of the flagged Pennine Way and field paths, some potentially muddy.

Car Parking: Pay and display car park by the National Park centre at the former railway station in Hawes. Grid reference: 875899

Map: Ordnance Survey Outdoor Leisure No. 30 – Yorkshire Dales, Northern and Central areas. 1:25000. (A Hawes and district local map to the same scale is available at the National Park Centre)

Description

This interesting circuit takes in the attractive little town of Hawes, solidly stone-built high in Wensleydale and the adjacent villages of Gayle, Appersett and Hardraw, linking them by the use of field paths and quiet lanes. The well-known and impressive Hardraw Force is England's highest single drop waterfall, at nearly 100 feet, and is only a short detour from the route. Views are extensive and varied throughout.

Hawes gradually usurped Askrigg as the main centre for Upper Wensleydale following receipt of a market charter in 1699 and the arrival of the turnpike road a few years later. Textile mills and quarrying were developed around the town, while the old hand-knitting industry continued. Its present day importance is confirmed by the establishment of a National Park centre, with local museum attached. Other attractions include rope and cheese manufacturing premises open for public visiting and a street market each Tuesday.

The Pennine Way passes through the town. Available accommodation includes a youth hostel and refreshments are available in Hawes itself and at Hardraw. Many of the town's historic and otherwise interesting buildings are listed in a small Hawes Town Trail booklet, obtainable locally.

Churchyard, Hawes

Route

From the car park cross the main road towards the post office and follow the street to the right, soon crossing the Gayle Beck, with its noisy little waterfall. Turn left up the steps in front of Herriot's Hotel to ascend moderately steeply towards the church. An open field is reached at a stile and gate. The flagged track ahead "Bealer Bank" is an old packhorse route, now part of the Pennine Way. The village of Gayle is in view, with some rather unattractive houses dominant. Better is the view of Gayle Mill and its weir to the left. This is a former cotton mill, built in 1787.

Turn left at the road, cross over and, in less than 100 yards turn right, still following "Pennine Way", between the houses, cross a field, and turn right at the lane. In about 50 yards turn right at a stile signposted to "Mossy Lane" and head for a further stile across a meadow. On reaching a farm building turn right at a gate at the far end, cross a beck on a plank bridge, pass through another gate, then a stile, followed by a diagonal ascent across a small field, where a stile gives access to a surfaced lane (Mossy Lane).

Turn right for 25 yards and then left at a stile signposted "Thorny Mire House ¾ mile". Cross a rising field to a stile, followed by a second stile close on the right, aiming to the left of a derelict building, then descending to a road, where a finger post marks the inevitable stile. Turn left, then right in 40 yards, to a bridleway signposted to Thorny Mire House. The track is now more obvious on the ground as it rises gently, bending left by the corner of a wall.

A long section between widely spaced walls follows, along the top of a steepish slope with fine views across the wide dale to the north, with Hardraw Scar rising high above Hardraw village. Closer at hand is bleak, raw, marginal farming country with the growth of rushes revealing a great deal of badly drained land. As Thorny Mire House is approached, a few belts of trees break the harshness of the landscape. On reaching a surfaced lane, turn right to pass the house, and rise gently above Widdale, with the old Appersett railway viaduct in view. Follow the road downhill to Appersett, where the main valley road is joined. Turn sharp left over Appersett Bridge to head for New Bridge; the path runs behind the wall on the left of the road. Climb the ladder stile at New Bridge, cross the River Ure, and follow round to the left, turning right in 100 yards at the road junction, signposted to Hardraw and Askrigg.

Dales museum and centre : the former Hawes railway station

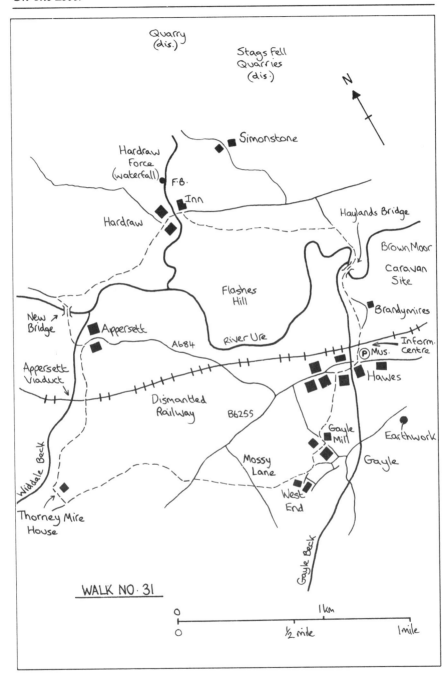

Quarry
(dis.)

Stags Fell
Quarries
(dis.)

N

Simonstone

Hardraw
Force
(waterfall)   F.B.

Inn

Hardraw

Haylands Bridge

Brown Moor

Caravan
Site

Flashes
Hill

New
Bridge

Appersett

Brandymires

A684

River Ure

Inform.
Centre

Appersett
Viaduct

P   Mus.

Hawes

Dismantled
Railway

B6255

Gayle
Mill

Earthwork

Gayle

Mossy
Lane

Widdale Beck

West
End

Thorney Mire
House

Gayle Beck

WALK NO. 31

0   1 Km

0   ½ mile   1 mile

The road climbs moderately at first, before dropping to Hardraw where an inn and two tea rooms offer refreshments as the Pennine Way is rejoined.

The celebrated falls are worth the short detour even though it does mean paying to use the only access – via the bar of the Green Dragon Inn!

From Hardraw turn right immediately after crossing the beck and follow the Pennine Way, signposted to "Brunt Acres Road", bearing left after passing the buildings on to a flagged track which is well-marked all the way to the road and is sufficiently elevated to have good views across the valley to Hawes, with the rather curious mound of Floshes Hill surrounded by water on three sides. Turn right at the road to head for Hawes. The river is crossed by a substantial bridge, soon followed by a kissing gate on the right giving access to a signposted short cut across a field, rejoining the road for return over the old railway bridge to the car park.

32

Wether Fell and the Roman road

Length: 5¼ miles

Rise and Fall: A little more than 300 feet in total. About half of this rise is very steady, along the Cam High Road. There is a fairly sharp ascent after the junction of paths and then short ups and downs around the flank of Wether Fell.

Underfoot: Very sharply divided. The Cam High Road is excellent; the subsequent path is varied, with parts peaty and likely to be wet at virtually any time of year.

Car Parking: The Cam High Road joins the Hawes to Kettlewell road high on the shoulder of the hill. Close to this point there are roadside spaces, both on the surfaced road and on the Cam High Road itself. Beware of obstructing the latter! Grid reference: 863854.

Map: Ordnance Survey Outdoor Leisure No. 30 Yorkshire Dales, Northern and Central areas. 1 : 25000

Description

In suggesting "level" routes for walkers, I have always promised that mountains and hills will not be climbed. In circumnavigating Wether Fell, this walk comes within a whisker of breaching that promise; indeed, a visit to the summit is suggested as a possible diversion. Having put those particular cards on the table, I must say that even "level" walkers must from time to time yearn for high places and the forethought of the Romans in providing this road gives the rare opportunity for the enjoyment of a real upland walk at a very modest overall cost in ascent, none of which is really steep.

The absence of steep hills should not automatically be interpreted as "easy" walk. The footpath part of this route is quite demanding in effort, particularly if the weather is unfavourable – high wind, saturated ground, rain or snow. The Cam High Road was constructed by the Romans to connect the fort at Bainbridge with Ingleton. Much later it was used as a drove road, and then became the first Richmond to Lancaster turnpike in 1751, being superseded by a road up Widdale, on the line of the present road, in 1795.

With such fascinating history under the boot soles, enjoyment of the splendid views can almost be regarded as a bonus.

Route

Start along the Cam High Road, a broad, generally stony track rising gently towards Wether Fell. The road is by no means as straight as is normally expected of a Roman road, but is of constant width, largely bounded by stone walls. Quite apart from the feeling of layers of history beneath one's feet, the road is a fine route for those who enjoy the sheer exhilaration of upland walking; the feeling of space, views for miles in several directions, clear fresh air, and few other people about.

The rather desolate valley of Sleddale is below on the left, but as progress is made Raydale comes into view on the right, with Semerwater visible under the unmistakeable step-ended mound of Addlebrough.

After passing the highest part of Wether Fell, just by the corner of a wall, turn left through a gap in that wall to follow a barely distinct grassy path. On reaching a gap in a partially broken stone wall, a decision must be made. The path continues to descend to meet another path rising from Burtersett. At that point a sharp left turn is made, followed by a longish ascent. The alternative is to avoid losing height by bearing left across roughish ground to meet the new path, avoiding most of the ascent.

Cam High Road, the Roman road above Hawes

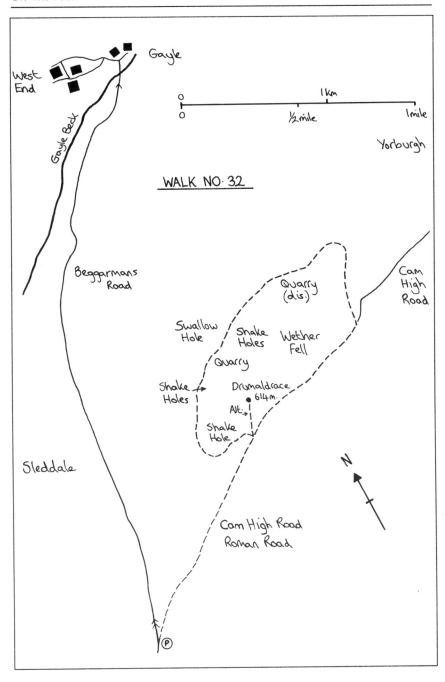

West End

Gayle

Gayle Beck

Yorburgh

0 ———— 1 Km
0 ———— ½ mile ———— 1 mile

WALK NO. 32

Beggarmans Road

Cam High Road

Quarry (dis.)

Swallow Hole

Shake Holes

Wether Fell

Quarry

Shake Holes

Drumaldrace
● 614m.

Alt:

Shake Hole

Sleddale

N

Cam High Road
Roman Road

P

In either case, follow this path to a gap in another wall. At this point the Ordnance Survey shows the path as heading straight on, later making a sharp right turn. This is not recommended as it leads directly into virtually impassable peat bogs. Instead, bear right to keep fairly close to a stone wall. This wall is an infallible guide to the next $1\frac{1}{3}$ miles around the flank of Wether Fell. The path maintains much the same overall level and is always distinct as it rises and falls from time to time, sometimes pleasant underfoot, sometimes awkward over boggy or peaty ground; shake holes are plentiful along the way. One section has views right across Wensleydale.

The Cam High Road is rejoined by the angle of a wall. The highest point of Wether Fell, named Drumaldrace on the map, is only 110 feet above and is probably best climbed from this point by those with energy still to expend. With or without this excursion, return along the road to the parking area.

Also of Interest:

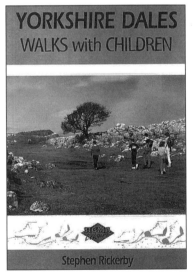

THE ABBEY TRAIL: Over 100 miles of walks through Yorkshire's finest countryside
Clive Newsome
An eight-day long-distance walk (with alternative circular day walks) visiting some of England's greatest abbeys. Brief histories are provided for all places along the trail and detailed maps clearly outline all routes adding to the enjoyment. The Yorkshire countryside with its gently sloping hills and valleys make it ideal for walkers of all ages and abilities. *£6.95*

BATTLEFIELD WALKS IN YORKSHIRE
David Clark
Be transported back in time with these detailed accounts of historic Yorkshire battles. Discover sites of 23 famous battles between 633 and 1945. Enjoy excellent walks in captivating scenery, each one including up-to-date information on access and facilities available in this beautiful region. *£6.95*

YORKSHIRE DALES WALKS WITH CHILDREN
Stephen Rickerby
Packed with interest and information for youngsters, this is the first book of walks in the Yorkshire Dales specifically aimed at parents and children. On these 21 circular routes – each less than 5 miles long – you'll find that children actually want to join you! *£6.95*

BY-WAY BIKING ON THE NORTH YORK MOORS
Roy Coleman
Explore the North York Moors National Park with these 20 varied circular routes presented in a unique format that makes it almost impossible to get lost! All come complete with Tea Room or Pub to stop off at en-route – enjoy the rides, don't endure them! *£7.95*

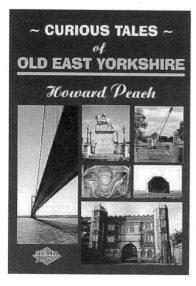

CURIOUS TALES OF OLD EAST YORKSHIRE
Howard Peach

An entertaining guide to the history, folklore, traditions and social institutions of the Old East Riding, arranged in fourteen diverse chapters. Its scope is wide-ranging, seriously researched and well illustrated – bringing a heightened appreciation of the rich heritage of East Yorkshire. Foreword by David Davis, MP for Cottingham. *£7.95*

CURIOUS TALES OF OLD NORTH YORKSHIRE
Howard Peach

More 'Curious Tales', this time for the old North Riding. An extraordinary compendium of detail in one book. People, legends, customs, romance and marriage, plus anecdotes not previously publicised. *£8.95*

STRANGE WORLD OF THE BRONTËS
Marie Campbell

A unique look at the little-known and forgotten facts relating to the Brontës and their part of West Yorkshire. Includes new and little known material concerning the involvement of the Brontës with occult practices. *£9.95*

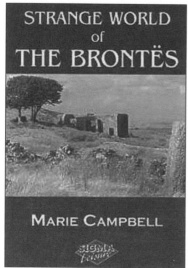